P9-CRK-351

# This Book Comes With Lots of
# FREE Online Resources

Nolo's award-winning website has a page dedicated just to this book. Here you can:

**KEEP UP TO DATE.** When there are important changes to the information in this book, we'll post updates.

**GET DISCOUNTS ON NOLO PRODUCTS.** Get discounts on hundreds of books, forms, and software.

**READ BLOGS.** Get the latest info from Nolo authors' blogs.

**LISTEN TO PODCASTS.** Listen to authors discuss timely issues on topics that interest you.

**WATCH VIDEOS.** Get a quick introduction to a legal topic with our short videos.

**And that's not all.**
Nolo.com contains thousands of articles on everyday legal and business issues, plus a plain-English law dictionary, all written by Nolo experts and available for free. You'll also find more useful **books, software, online apps, downloadable forms,** plus a **lawyer directory.**

## 9th Edition

# Nolo's Quick LLC

Attorney Anthony Mancuso

| NINTH EDITION | FEBRUARY 2017 |
|---|---|
| Editor | BETH LAURENCE |
| Cover Design | SUSAN PUTNEY |
| Book Production | SUSAN PUTNEY |
| Proofreader | ROBERT WELLS |
| Index | ACCESS POINTS INDEXING |
| Printer | BANG PRINTING |

ISSN: 1932-1740 (print)
ISSN: 2375-2858 (online)
ISBN: 978-1-4133-2347-4 (pbk)
ISBN: 978-1-4133-2348-1 (epub ebook)

This book covers only United States law, unless it specifically states otherwise.

### Please note

We believe accurate, plain-English legal information should help you solve many of your own legal problems. But this text is not a substitute for personalized advice from a knowledgeable lawyer. If you want the help of a trained professional—and we'll always point out situations in which we think that's a good idea—consult an attorney licensed to practice in your state.

## Acknowledgments

A special thanks to Beth Laurence, my editor, and to all the Noloids at Nolo for their continued assistance in helping me produce another self-help law business resource.

## About the Author

Anthony Mancuso is a California attorney and a corporations and limited liability company expert. He graduated from Hastings College of the Law in San Francisco, is a member of the California State Bar, writes books and software in the fields of corporate and LLC law, and has studied advanced business taxation at Golden Gate University in San Francisco. He also works as a technical writer and programmer and is currently employed by Google in Mountain View, California. He is the author of many Nolo books on forming and operating corporations (both profit and nonprofit) and limited liability companies. His titles include *Incorporate Your Business: A Legal Guide to Forming a Corporation in Your State*, *How to Form a Nonprofit Corporation* (national and California editions), *Form Your Own Limited Liability Company*, *The Corporate Records Handbook: Meetings, Minutes & Resolutions*, *LLC or Corporation? How to Choose the Right Form for Your Business*, and *Your Limited Liability Company: An Operating Manual*. His books have shown over a quarter of a million businesses and organizations how to form a corporation or LLC. He also is a licensed helicopter pilot and has performed for years as a guitarist.

# Table of Contents

# Appendixes

# Introduction

n the business world, limited liability companies are seen as the latest hot thing. The limited liability company (LLC) is a relatively new business ownership structure that combines the best features of the corporation and the partnership. It gives small business owners corporate-style protection from personal liability while retaining the pass-through income tax treatment enjoyed by sole proprietorships (the legal term for one-person businesses) and partnerships.

Protection from personal liability—often referred to as "limited liability"—means that creditors of the business cannot normally go after the owners' personal assets to pay LLC debts and claims arising from lawsuits; pass-through tax treatment means that business profits are reported and taxed on the individual income tax returns of the business owners. I'll discuss limited liability and pass-through taxation in much more depth in Chapter 1.

All 50 states and the District of Columbia now allow people to form this unique type of legal and tax entity, and most make it easy, convenient, and even relatively economical for small business owners to create and register an LLC. For these reasons, more and more entrepreneurs are choosing to organize their businesses as LLCs. And there have been three relatively recent developments that have added fuel to the LLC fire:

- Tough economic times have made it more important than ever for business owners to limit their liability for business debts, either by forming an LLC in the first place or by converting an existing sole proprietorship or partnership to an LLC. If an LLC falls behind on its bills, creditors know that their only legal remedy is against the business, not against the owner personally. This gives creditors a strong incentive to work with the owner to settle outstanding accounts. Even if the worst-case scenario comes to pass and the business fails, at least the owner won't be personally liable for its debts.

- All states now permit single-owner LLCs. This means that a person who has done business in the past as a sole proprietor (or is just starting out) can now protect his or her personal assets from business debts and claims by filing some simple paperwork and forming an LLC.

- The IRS now allows LLCs (including single-owner LLCs) to choose between pass-through taxation and corporate tax treatment. Although most LLC owners will decide to stick with pass-through tax status (paying tax on their individual income tax returns), they can also elect to be taxed as a corporation, splitting business income between the business and their own personal income tax returns, which can lower overall business income taxes. As you'll see in Chapter 4, income splitting can make sense for LLCs that make more than the owners want to take out of the business or that need to retain substantial profits on a regular basis.

For me, the most convincing evidence that the LLC has indeed caught on as a popular small business legal entity is the fact that, almost every day, I notice more small businesses with the telltale "LLC" tag at the end of their business names. If you doubt this, just enter any big office building and look at the directory of tenants: You're bound to notice a good sprinkling of LLC business names along with the traditional "Inc." and "Corp." designators.

## Should You Consider Forming an LLC?

Forming a new business as an LLC is an easy, quick, and relatively inexpensive way for new business owners to operate a business with limited liability while paying taxes on their individual income tax returns. Likewise, converting an existing sole proprietorship or partnership to an LLC is an easy way for sole proprietors and partners to protect their personal assets without changing the income tax treatment of their business.

But this doesn't address the larger question: Does it make sense for you to form your new business as an LLC—or to convert your existing business into an LLC? Unless you have already incorporated or you run a microbusiness that has little chance of incurring debts or liabilities, my answer is simple: Yes, you probably should form an LLC. Here's why: Forming an LLC is very easy—you just fill in a standard form provided by most state LLC filing offices and file it, usually for a modest filing fee. And in exchange for your small efforts, you will receive a big legal benefit—your personal assets will be protected from business debts and claims, without making your taxes more complicated.

A few examples help to illustrate when it does and doesn't make sense to form an LLC:

EXAMPLE 1: Sam sets up a music store to sell guitars, keyboards, and musical accessories. Because members of the public will enter his retail space, Sam has some potential legal exposure (slip-and-fall lawsuits, for example). In addition, he knows that it's easy to become enmeshed in contract disputes with suppliers and customers (for example, buyer's remorse can often set in shortly after the purchase of a pricey guitar or synthesizer). Even though Sam will carry a reasonable amount of commercial liability insurance and do his best to keep his customers satisfied, he decides that it makes sense to file LLC articles of organization with his state for a $125 fee, so he can take advantage of the extra personal security that limited liability protection affords. Sam's state, like many others, also charges a $50 annual report fee each year, but aside from this small expense and the few minutes it takes to complete the simple one-page annual filing form, there are very few added costs or burdens associated with doing business as an LLC. And Sam knows that by forming an LLC instead of operating as a sole proprietor, he won't get a different tax status, as he would if he elected to form a corporation (the other legal entity that provides owners with limited personal liability for business debts).

EXAMPLE 2: Stella and Vera have operated a pet grooming business from rented quarters in a strip mall for several years. Their partnership has been successful, and they've managed to increase their profits every year. Of course, there have been small problems with the occasional fussy pet owner—and they were sued once in small claims court for a poodle dye-job that went slightly awry—but no big lawsuits or other major legal hassles. However, as profits have grown, so too have the owners' worries about their business. They are a lot busier than they used to be, and have had to hire several employees. They know that although their employees are well trained, expensive mistakes can happen, especially when new people come on board. Stella and Vera have also begun to worry about employee lawsuits. If the owners have to fire someone, will the employee go quietly or hire a lawyer and make their lives miserable for a while?

Because of these concerns, Stella and Vera decide to turn their partnership into an LLC. They do this by filing a one-page "Conversion of Partnership to an LLC" form, provided by their state. The filing fee is small, and they still file taxes as if they were a partnership (each owner continues to report and pay taxes on her share of business profits on her 1040 individual income tax return, and the business continues to file IRS Form 1065, an informational tax return for partnerships). Now both Stella and Vera rest a little easier at the end of each pet-grooming day, knowing that they won't be personally liable for any legal problems they face in the future of their business. Of course, because the assets of their business remain at stake (as opposed to their personal assets), Stella and Vera will continue to choose and train their employees carefully.

CAUTION

**Not all states provide a form for converting from a partnership to an LLC.** In states that don't provide a conversion form, partners file regular articles of organization to create their LLC. In some states, they also have to publish a notice in a local newspaper that they are terminating their partnership. I discuss these requirements in Chapter 6.

EXAMPLE 3: Winston is a graphic artist, sitting 40 hours per week in his well-lit cubicle, churning out computer art for a software publishing firm. He yearns for the day when he can work for, and answer only to, himself in his own computer-graphics business. Rather than just quit his day job cold turkey, Winston starts his new business by working from home in the evenings and on weekends doing 3-D animation. Winston does most of his projects on a work-for-hire basis for Bill, a good friend of Winston's and an entrepreneur who recently started a video game software company. Winston likes the fact that his animation work is fun, but he loves the fact that he can bill his services at an hourly rate that is twice what he makes at his day job.

Winston has heard about the advantages of forming an LLC, but he decides not to form one for his moonlighting business, at least for the time being. His reasons are:

- He doesn't feel that his sideline business exposes him to personal liability since he works at home, under the terms of a very basic work-for-hire agreement with Bill, who pays Winston's invoices on time every time.
- He is too busy with his regular job and his new business to concentrate on the legal end of his business.

Winston's decision is a sensible one. Even though converting a sole proprietorship to an LLC isn't difficult, Winston doesn't need to take this step yet. If Winston continues to operate as a sole proprietor (as most freelancers do), he doesn't need to keep his personal funds and business funds separate. If Winston were to form an LLC, he would need to keep his personal funds separate from his business funds (to be sure that a court will respect the separate legal existence of his LLC, and its limited liability protection). And, if he decides to stop moonlighting, all he has to do is stop working. Forming an LLC, no matter how easy, will make Winston's business life more formal, and if he goes on to something else, he will have to officially dissolve his LLC. This is a little more trouble than just doing business as a sole proprietorship.

EXAMPLE 4. Bill, Winston's only client, has just started his own video game software venture, as mentioned in the above example. Bill knows that forming an LLC is a modern legal strategy, and he is definitely a cutting edge kind of guy. His plans are big—he hopes to hire a crew of talented programmers from the local college, then turn them loose to create the latest in 3-D video game software. He can't pay his software team much to start, but he thinks he can convince them of the profit-making potential of the enterprise, particularly if one of the company's software offerings gets licensed by one of the big video game companies. He's sure his company has a good chance of success, but he also wants to limit his personal liability in case something goes wrong (for instance, if his company folds while owing money to creditors).

Bill considers forming an LLC, but decides to form a corporation instead. The corporation will give him the same limited liability protection an LLC affords, but it offers Bill some special advantages that suit his business plan better. With a corporation, Bill can attract employees by offering them stock options—which, despite the fluctuations in the stock market, are considered desirable by employees in companies that have the potential to go public or be acquired for big bucks. Also, after reading Chapter 2 of this book, Bill understands that forming a corporation is often the best approach for attracting outside investors. This is important to Bill, who plans to do a lot of networking to find a venture capital firm to help fund the growth of his business. With a corporation, Bill can offer investors stock ownership and a seat on the board of directors.

Even though a corporation requires much more work to maintain—you will have to hold annual and special directors' and shareholders' meetings, plus keep a more complicated set of accounting records for the business and prepare a separate income tax return—incorporating makes sense for Bill. While an LLC insulates the personal assets of owners of a small, privately held business venture, sometimes it's not a good vehicle for outside investors like venture capitalists. Let's take a look at the reasons.

An LLC can be set up with a management structure that has the same centralized features as a board-managed corporation—for example, the LLC can select a management team consisting of owners who are active in the business and possibly an outside investor (see Chapters 1 and 5 for a discussion of LLC management). But precisely because LLCs are more flexible and informal business entities, they can be less disciplined and less responsive to the interests of outside investors. LLCs don't provide as many management protections and controls as corporations, such as shareholder inspection rights and annual disclosure requirements, which makes it more difficult for investors to hold management accountable.

In addition, it's more difficult to set up different classes of ownership in an LLC to cater to the special concerns of investors. In contrast, in a corporation, the founders can adopt an off-the-shelf capitalization structure of nonpreferred and preferred shares—which are usually immediately attractive to venture capital investors. And forget about taking an LLC public with an IPO (initial public offering of stock)—if this is your short-term dream, you'll no doubt want to incorporate to take advantage of the long-established statutory procedures for attracting and maintaining a large group of investors (shareholders).

> **CAUTION**
>
> **Most small businesses don't want to incorporate.** Because a corporation limits its owners' personal liability for business debts, and because, unlike LLCs, corporations have been around for centuries, people often ask if it makes more sense to incorporate. The answer is most often "No" unless, as discussed just above, there is a really good reason to incorporate, such as wanting to sell stock to investors or distribute stock options to employees. For most other small businesses—those that are owned by just a few people and have no plans to go public—forming an LLC is usually the best approach, because LLCs also offer limited liability protection, and corporations are considerably harder to maintain. For example, state corporate statutes have specific rules for holding meetings of directors and shareholders, issuing stock, distributing profits, and much more. Also, unlike an LLC, a corporation is a

separate tax entity that calculates profits according to a lot of special corporate tax rules and then reports and pays taxes on these profits separately from its owners. While LLCs have the option to elect this added income tax complexity, they can wait until the owners decide that it makes tax sense to do so. (I discuss electing corporate tax treatment in Chapter 4.)

Don't worry if you still don't know whether an LLC is right for you. By reading the rest of this book, you'll understand better the features of an LLC and how they can work for you. Also, in Appendix C, I've provided a checklist for forming an LLC, which includes a list of questions to help you decide whether it makes sense to run your business as an LLC.

CAUTION
**Some types of businesses cannot form an LLC.** Banking, trust, or insurance businesses are prohibited from forming LLCs in many states. In addition, some states also prohibit certain professionals (or anyone holding a vocational license) from forming an LLC, or at least subject them to special rules when forming one. (For example, professionals may need to form a professional LLC or they may need to get prior approval from their licensing board to do business as an LLC.) If you fall into one of these categories, take a minute to skip ahead to Chapter 1 to see whether you'll be eligible to form an LLC.

## How to Use This Book

In this book, I provide basic legal and tax information about LLCs. My purpose is to help you understand exactly where LLCs fit into the larger picture of business ownership structures and to help you decide whether it makes sense for you to form an LLC to conduct your business.

Because many busy people won't have time to read this book from cover to cover, I do my best to provide this information in a well-organized, easy-to-access format. First, I suggest you read Chapter 1 to get a good overview of how LLCs work. Then, to find the exact material you're interested in, look at the chapter subheadings in the table of contents. (These are repeated at the start of each chapter.) Each time you pick up the book to read a different section, your "LLC IQ" will increase and, within a short time, you'll know enough to decide if the LLC business structure might be a good fit for you and your business.

Another reason why I take this practical approach is philosophical. A major attraction of the LLC is that you can form one simply, quickly, and with a lot of flexibility. It follows that a book that provides an overview of LLCs should fit this same model. The idea is to use it quickly to get the information you need and then get back to business. And, let's be honest—if you are going to spend leisure time curled up with a book, I'm sure you can think of several with better plotlines and character development.

## What This Book Doesn't Do

You can't form an LLC using this book alone. Its goal is to provide a good overview of the subject, no more. So if you already know a good deal about LLC legalities and tax issues, including how LLCs are formed and operated, you may want to get right to the task of forming one. If so, my other Nolo books and products can help you do the job. See "Other Nolo LLC Resources," below, for more information.

## Legal and Tax Experts

This book provides basic legal and tax information. As in any other specialized field, LLC legal and tax information constantly changes. If you decide you want to form an LLC, you will benefit by discussing your specific situation with a small business lawyer and/or a small business tax adviser. Not only can professional advisers make sure you have the most current information on forming an LLC in your state, but they can also serve as great sounding boards to check your legal, tax, and practical conclusions. In Chapter 7, I provide several recommendations on how to find knowledgeable and helpful legal and tax advisers.

# Other Nolo LLC Resources

Below is a list of Nolo resources that can help you actually form and operate an LLC. Of course, these are not the only helpful products on the market—they're just the ones I know best (after all, I wrote or created most of them!). All are available at Nolo's website (www.nolo.com).

- *LLC or Corporation? How to Choose the Right Form for Your Business*, by Anthony Mancuso. This companion to *Nolo's Quick LLC* explains in detail the technical legal and tax differences between LLCs and corporations. It also provides more detailed information on the legal and tax consequences of converting a business to (or from) an LLC or a corporation.

- *Form Your Own Limited Liability Company*, by Anthony Mancuso. This book contains forms and instructions for preparing articles of organization (the main organizational document for LLCs) and an operating agreement (similar to corporate bylaws) to form an LLC in your state. It also provides legal and tax background information.

- Nolo's online LLC formation service. To create your LLC right now, use Nolo's online service, which helps you form your LLC directly on the Internet. Once you pick a package and complete an interview online, Nolo will create a customized LLC operating agreement for your LLC and file your articles of organization with the state filing office. (Your LLC will come into existence the day the articles are filed.) To form your LLC online or get more information, go to www.nolo.com/online-LLC.

- *Your Limited Liability Company: An Operating Manual*, by Anthony Mancuso. This post-start-up book provides guidance and information on how to best operate your LLC on an ongoing basis. It provides ready-to-use minutes forms and instructions for holding formal LLC meetings. It also advises you on how to formally approve legal, tax, and other important business decisions that arise in the course of operating an LLC, and includes resolution forms to record these decisions.

- *Business Buyout Agreements: Plan Now for Retirement, Death, Divorce or Owner Disagreements*, by Anthony Mancuso and Bethany K. Laurence. This book shows you how to adopt comprehensive provisions to handle the purchase and sale of ownership interests in an LLC when an owner withdraws, dies, becomes disabled, or wishes to sell his or her interest to an outsider. Comes with an easy-to-use agreement—you simply check the appropriate options, then fill in the blanks.
- *Tax Savvy for Small Business*, by Frederick W. Daily and Jeffrey A. Quinn. This book gives LLC owners information about federal taxes and explains how to make the best tax decisions for your business, maximize profits, and stay out of trouble with the IRS.

---

### Get Updates to This Book and More on Nolo.com

When there are important changes to the information in this book, we'll post updates online, on a page dedicated to this book:

**www.nolo.com/back-of-book/LLCQ.html**

You'll find other useful information there, too, including author blogs, podcasts, and videos.

---

# An Overview of LLCs

The LLC is a relatively new and highly popular alternative to the five traditional ways of doing business: as a sole proprietor, a general partnership, a limited partnership, a C (regular) corporation, and an S corporation. In this book I'll explain not only how LLCs work and why they're so popular, but also how the LLC compares to each of these other business forms (see Chapter 2).

By and large, the business media have heralded the arrival of the LLC with unabated enthusiasm. And, in my opinion, this fanfare is justified. The LLC is the first business ownership structure that allows all owners of the business to quickly and easily achieve the dual goals of "pass-through" tax treatment (the same tax treatment sole proprietors and partnerships receive) and limited personal liability protection.

## Basic LLC Features

Now let's look more closely at the specific legal and tax characteristics that make the LLC so attractive and set it apart from the other business ownership structures. As you'll see in Chapter 2, most of the LLC's characteristics are shared by at least some of the other business structures. What makes the LLC unique is that it's the only business entity with its particular mix of legal and tax attributes—most importantly, limited personal liability for LLC owners (the same legal protection that owners of a corporation enjoy) and pass-through taxation (like sole proprietors or the owners of a partnership). The legislators who thought up the LLC business structure were smart enough to realize that there was no need to reinvent the wheel—all they had to do was combine the best legal and tax aspects of the corporation and the partnership.

## A Very Short History of the LLC

The LLC is the American version of a type of business organization that has existed for years in other countries. Specifically, it closely resembles the German *GmbH*, the French *SARL*, and the South American *Limitada* forms of doing business, all of which allow small groups of individuals to enjoy limited personal liability while avoiding the more complex tax rules that apply to corporations.

In the U.S., the Wyoming legislature enacted the first LLC legislation in 1977, followed by Florida in 1982. In those days, doing business as an LLC was risky, in part because the IRS had not yet made it clear whether it would tax an LLC as a partnership or a corporation. In fact, because the central promise of the LLC—to enjoy the tax status of a partnership with the personal liability protection of a corporation—seemed almost too good to be true, few business owners were brave enough to avail themselves of this new business model. And most other states were unwilling to pass legislation authorizing LLCs until the IRS gave its approval.

The first big break in the LLC stalemate came in 1988, when the IRS ruled that an LLC formed under the Wyoming statute was eligible for pass-through tax status. This nod of approval from the IRS created an immediate national wave of enthusiasm for LLCs in the business press, and all 50 states plus the District of Columbia quickly adopted LLC legislation.

But it wasn't until January 1, 1997 that LLCs really went mainstream. That's when the IRS threw out its old and unnecessarily complicated tax classification regulations, agreeing that multi-owner LLCs could henceforth enjoy partnership tax status (and that one-owner LLCs could be taxed as sole proprietors) without the need to jump through a bunch of previously required technical hoops. Even better, the IRS also decided to give LLC owners the flexibility to change their tax status by electing corporate tax treatment if they wish. (Chapter 4 explains this option.)

## Number of Owners (Members)

Contrary to what you may have read just a few years ago, you can now form an LLC with just one person in any state (or the District of Columbia).

While there's no maximum number of owners (legally called "members") an LLC can have, for practical reasons you'll probably want to keep the group reasonably small. There's no magic number here, but any business that's actively owned and operated by more than about five people risks serious problems maintaining good communication and reaching consensus among the owners.

Of course, if some of your co-owners will be passive investors only—and you'll have a small management group calling the day-to-day shots—you can sensibly consider having more owners. (See "Flexible Management Structure," below, for more on this type of arrangement.) But I still think there is a commonsense limit to the total number of members (including active owners and inactive investors). In my experience, once you get more than about ten investors, you'll find that accounting and communication issues are likely to use up too much of your time. Outside investors will want to stay informed and may make your business life more complicated if your management choices do not result in increasing profits in future years. Also, the larger your investor group grows, the more likely you are to run into securities law complexities (see Chapter 6 for more on this).

## Limited Personal Liability Protection

The owners of an LLC are not personally liable for the debts of their business or claims made against it (with a few exceptions, discussed in "Exceptions to Owners' Limited Liability," below). This legal protection is written into each state's LLC law. Because almost every business will accumulate debts and face some risk of being sued, this is a popular—and valuable—feature. Without limited personal liability, all business owners are 100% legally responsible to repay these debts, even if they have to use their own money. With limited liability, their personal assets should remain untouched, even if the business fails under a heavy weight of debts and judgments.

| How a Business Can Go Into Debt |
|---|
| Businesses accumulate debt as a routine part of their activities. For example, when sales or net profits are low, employees, suppliers, and other routine business expenses must still be paid. In times like these, a business might take out a loan or use a line of credit with a bank to handle cash flow fluctuations and pay bills. Many businesses also defer payment of expenses by buying needed materials and supplies from vendors on account (usually with a 30- to 90-day grace period to pay these balances). In short, there are many reasons why a company, even a successful one, might take on debt as it transacts business. |

EXAMPLE 1: George and Vera quit their day jobs to go into business for themselves. They plan to sell a new brand of wireless modem under an exclusive distributorship license with the modem manufacturer. They believe they can ultimately develop a large repeat-customer base of consumers who are looking for the latest, easiest way to connect to the Internet. George and Vera realize, however, that it will be slow going at the start of their new venture, which makes them worry about what will happen if they are not able to resell all the modems they have to buy up front to qualify for their distributorship license. In a worst-case scenario, they might even have to close their new business. While they are ready to accept the risk of their business failing, they are frightened that they could run up so much debt that they might have to sell their personal assets to pay it off, or even declare bankruptcy.

If George and Vera operated their business as a partnership, they would be right to worry, because any debts their business takes on would automatically become their personal debts. But if George and Vera instead form an LLC, they'll have a lot less to worry about. If their business idea does not succeed, their business debts will not become their personal debts. As long as George and Vera do not personally guarantee (cosign for) any debts of their LLC, they are simply not on the hook for debts the business cannot repay. They'll be able to go back to their unforeclosed-upon houses, reapply for their day jobs, and start building their dreams and fortunes again.

TIP
**Commercial insurance doesn't cover business debts.** While commercial insurance can protect a business and its owners from some types of liability (for instance, slip-and-fall lawsuits), insurance never covers business debts. The only way to limit your personal liability for business debts is to use a limited liability business structure such as an LLC, a corporation, a limited partnership, or a registered limited liability partnership (RLLP), which I discuss in Chapter 2.

EXAMPLE 2: Zena forms her own one-person mail-order business, "Personal Goddess Boutiques," consisting of a specialty catalog she plans to distribute to women with lots of disposable income. Her catalog will include inexpensive as well as high-priced items, such as luxury cruises, spa accommodations, and even resort-area luxury condos. Zena, who has an MBA and has built up an impressive résumé of past experience in travel agencies, luxury resorts, and retail sales, knows she will have to use most of her $250,000 in savings to buy mailing lists, establish a website, and otherwise reach her projected customer base. She hopes to buy or arrange for the purchase of much of her catalog inventory on a consignment or commission basis, thus minimizing her risk of overstocking inventory. Still, she knows that she will have to buy a significant portion of her sales inventory, and that many of these luxury items will be nonreturnable if they can't be sold.

Another area of financial exposure is the service package part of her business. She knows from experience that disgruntled clients might refuse to pay for packages (or demand a refund) for all sorts of good and bad reasons. In addition, while Zena is excited about the prospects for her new business, she also realizes that her business will be vulnerable to all sorts of problems in its early years. While she is willing to risk her $250,000 investment to pursue her dream, she is worried that if Personal Goddess fails, she will be buried under a pile of debt. Zena decides to form an LLC, with herself as the only owner. She feels a lot better going into business knowing that even under the worst possible scenario she can walk away without risking her personal assets.

## Flexible Capital Structure

In addition to limited personal liability, LLC owners (members) enjoy the benefits of a structure that allows great ownership flexibility. Let's start with the basics. Owners of an LLC invest money or property in the LLC in return for a capital interest in the form of an undivided percentage of the assets of the company. A member's capital interest is often represented by a certain amount of "membership units," much like shares in a corporation. For instance, a member who owns one-half of an LLC may own 500,000 out of a total one million membership units. In other instances, an LLC won't break down a capital interest into membership units, but will just say a one-half owner has a 50% capital interest. Either way, each owner's ownership percentage (capital interest) is used to divide LLC assets among the members if the LLC is sold or liquidated, or when a member wishes to sell a membership interest. The owners' relative percentages of ownership also can be used—but do not have to be—to calculate how to divide profits and losses of the LLC, and for other purposes (for example, to apportion LLC management voting power).

EXAMPLE 1: Three people form an LLC. Two combine to contribute half the cash and property used to set up the LLC, the third invests the other half. Under a typical ownership scenario, the first two members each get a 25% capital interest in the LLC; the third member gets a 50% interest. Under standard provisions of an LLC operating agreement, the members would be allocated a corresponding percentage of LLC profits and losses. That is, each 25% member would be allocated 25% of the LLC's profits and losses, and the 50% member would be allocated 50%. Also, if one of the members wishes to leave the LLC and sell his or her interest to the other members, the departing member can expect to receive a percentage of the current value of the LLC that corresponds to his or her capital interest percentage—a 25% member can expect to be paid 25% of the current value of the LLC.

EXAMPLE 2: Tasty Treats, LLC, is a neighborhood bakery owned by Ned, Sylvia, and four of their relatives. Only Ned and Sylvia work in the bakery. The LLC issues a total of 600,000 membership units to the initial investors. Under their LLC agreement, Ned and Sylvia, who contribute their know-how plus an investment of cash and property, get 200,000 membership units each; their relatives, each of whom makes a small cash investment, get 50,000 units each. If Ned were to resign from the LLC, he would get one-third of the value of the LLC (200,000/600,000). Likewise, if Ned and Sylvia were to decide to buy out their relatives, they could expect to pay one-third of the value of the LLC for all of their relatives' capital interests.

Assuming other members agree, in most states LLC members can contribute cash, property, services, or a promise to deliver any of the above, in exchange for capital interests in the LLC. While it's most common for all LLC members to contribute cash, it's not unusual for a member to also contribute a vehicle or a piece of equipment to the LLC. I discuss these various types of contributions (and the tax ramifications of each) in Chapter 3.

## Flexible Distribution of Profits and Losses

Many LLCs divide up profits and losses according to how much of the LLC each member owns. But they don't have to: LLC owners may choose to divide profits and losses any way they wish (subject to special IRS rules, which I discuss in Chapter 3). For example, if three equal LLC owners decide to divide profits 40%, 40%, and 20%, that's fine with the IRS, as long as they follow its rules and pay taxes on what they receive.

> EXAMPLE: Steve and Frankie form an educational seminar business, with each getting a one-half capital interest in the LLC. Steve puts up all the cash necessary to purchase a computer with graphics and multimedia presentation capabilities, rent out initial seminar sites, send out mass mailings, and purchase advertising. As the traveling lecturer and student pied piper, cash-poor Frankie will contribute only services to the LLC. (As explained in Chapter 3, Frankie will have to pay income tax on his one-half capital interest because it's a form of payment for his services.) Although the two owners could agree to split profits and losses equally (in proportion to their ownership interests), they decide that it's fair for Steve to get 65% of LLC profits for the first three years to pay him back for putting liquid assets (cash) into the LLC. After that, profits will be divided 50–50.

When it comes to actually paying out profits to the members, LLCs do have to pay attention to a few legal rules—in many states, there are financial standards that dictate when distributions can legally be made. I'll discuss these requirements in Chapter 4.

## Pass-Through Income Taxation of Profits and Losses

Like partnerships and sole proprietorships, an LLC is automatically recognized by the IRS as a "pass-through" tax entity. This term refers to the fact that all of the business's profits and losses "pass through" the business and are reflected and taxed on the owners' individual tax returns. (I discuss pass-through taxation fully in Chapter 4.) By contrast, the profits and losses of a corporation must be reported and taxed on a separate, corporate tax return, at special corporate income tax rates. And, of course, money paid to corporate owners by way of salaries, bonuses, and dividends is taxed on the owners' individual returns.

Why do many small business owners prefer pass-through taxation? For one, it's what most of us are used to. Every employee's salary is taxed this way, as are the profits earned by a sole proprietor or partnership.

Here's another reason: The alternative to pass-through taxation—corporate taxation—is too complicated for most small businesses, at least when the business is in its start-up phase. A corporation is treated as a separate taxable entity by the IRS, so it doesn't just pass its profits through to its owners. Instead, it pays tax on its own profits, and the owners pay tax on money the corporation pays them. Without going into the details, it's safe to say this means more bookkeeping, more accounting, and more complexity. (I explain corporate taxation in detail in Chapter 2.)

> ### TIP
> **An LLC can elect to be taxed as a corporation.** While most new LLCs will not choose to do so, a few will find that being taxed as a corporation actually reduces their tax bill. This might happen if an LLC wants or needs to keep some money in the business, rather than paying all of the profits out to the owners. The savings occur because corporate tax rates are initially lower than the individual rates that apply to most LLC owners.

Pass-through tax status also allows an LLC to pass business losses along to the owners to deduct from their other income (usually salary earned working for another company or income earned from investments). Many new businesses lose money in their first year or two. Fortunately, LLC members (like owners of partnerships) can subtract their LLC losses from their taxable income (assuming IRS rules are met).

## Flexible Management Structure

LLCs are managed by their members (known as *member management*) unless they choose to be managed by a manager or management group (known as *manager management*). LLCs with only a few members are almost always managed by all members—after all, most small business owners want to have an active hand in management. Fortunately for these LLCs, member management is simple and straightforward.

But member management isn't the best choice for all LLCs. Under the other option, manager management, an LLC is managed by a single manager or a small group of managers consisting of one or more selected LLC members, one or more nonmembers, or a mixture of the two. Manager management may make sense for an LLC in any of the following situations:

- One or more of the LLC members wants to invest in the LLC only, not help run it or take part in the management decisions.
- The LLC members wish to give an outsider (a nonmember) a vote in management. For example, an outsider might insist on having a say in management decisions in exchange for lending the LLC money. To give the nonmember management authority, the LLC must select manager management and create a management group that includes the outsider.
- The sole member of an LLC wants to manage the business but give membership interests to nonmanaging family members, who will step into a management role when the current owner-manager steps down.

Fortunately, an LLC can easily choose manager management to handle any of these situations. In most states, a short clause is included in the articles of organization (the paperwork filed with the state to form the LLC) saying that the LLC is managed by a manager or a group of managers. (A few states refer to managers as "governors.") In other states, the management structure of the LLC must be spelled out in the LLC operating agreement. (I discuss creating operating agreements, which are similar to corporate bylaws, in Chapter 6.)

Let's look at some management options for Ned and Sylvia's LLC, Tasty Treats, which I introduced in the example above.

> **EXAMPLE 1:** If Tasty Treats is set up with member management, all of the members, including Ned and Sylvia's investing relatives, manage the LLC. This may initially seem like an overly complex management structure; after all, Ned and Sylvia are the only two owners who work in the bakery. In practice, however, it probably won't be that complicated. The LLC operating agreement requires a full member vote only for major decisions, such as admitting a new member, selling a membership interest, incurring LLC debt outside the normal course of business operations, selling major LLC assets, dissolving the LLC, and the like. And these are exactly the types of big decisions these relatives want to be consulted on. Ned and Sylvia alone handle the day-to-day operation of the bakery and are allocated a guaranteed payout of LLC profits for their management duties, over and above their standard profit interest in the LLC.

> **EXAMPLE 2:** Now let's look at how things would work if Tasty Treats were organized as a manager-managed LLC. Assume Ned and Sylvia's relatives want no say in LLC business, which they invested in primarily to help out Ned and Sylvia. The relatives just want their share of annual LLC profits, and a proportionate percentage of the proceeds if it is later sold at a profit. The LLC elects manager management in its articles, and Ned and Sylvia are named as the LLC's two managers. In this operating scenario, only Ned and Sylvia vote when any of the decisions specified in the operating agreement must be made.

Of course, these examples outline two basic management styles. When it gets down to fine-print management provisions, there are numerous ways to set up the management of your LLC, whether you opt for a member-run or manager-run LLC. I discuss LLC management, decision making, and record keeping in more detail in Chapter 6.

# Exceptions to Owners' Limited Liability

While LLC owners enjoy limited personal liability for many of their business transactions, it is important to realize that this protection is not quite absolute. In several situations that I discuss below, an LLC owner may become personally liable for business debts or claims. This drawback is not unique to LLCs—many of these same exceptions apply to all limited liability business structures, including corporations. The limited liability protection held by LLC members is just as strong as that enjoyed by the corporate shareholders of small corporations. (To find out why, see "Losing Your Limited Liability," below.)

That said, let's look at the most common ways an owner might not be protected by limited liability.

## Personally Guaranteed Business Debts

No matter how a small business is organized, whether as an LLC, a partnership, or a corporation, its owners may be asked to sign bank loan obligations or to personally guarantee to pay business debts. Owners who agree to this voluntarily give up their limited liability protection as to these loans.

> EXAMPLE: A married couple owns and operates Books & Bagels, a coffee shop and bookstore. In need of dough (the green kind) to expand into a larger location, the owners ask a bank for a smallish loan. The bank grants the loan to the LLC on the condition that the two owners personally pledge their equity in their house as security for the loan. Because the owners personally guarantee the loan, if the LLC goes broke, the bank can seek repayment from the owners personally. If they can't come up with the cash, the bank could even foreclose on their house. No type of business ownership structure—an LLC, a corporation, or a limited partnership—can protect owners if they choose to assume personal liability.

But don't worry: Even if you have to personally cosign a business loan from time to time, there are plenty of other situations where your LLC's limited liability protection remains intact. That's because most of your business debts—and possibly even loans you negotiate with individuals—will not also be personal debts. For instance, your LLC's lines of credit with vendors and other suppliers and all its routine bills are debts of the LLC only, not personal debts of the LLC owners. In short, unless you go out of your way to pledge personal assets for business debts, you'll have no personal liability for them.

## Injuries to Others (Torts)

Like it or not, members and managers of an LLC, like corporate directors and shareholders, partners, and all other business owners, can be held personally liable for financial loss caused by their own careless behavior. Called "torts" in legalese, negligent acts (such as those that result in car crashes) are the everyday stuff of American litigation. But while an LLC member or manager is personally responsible for his or her own negligence (if the LLC can't or doesn't pay), the good news is that personal liability for torts does not typically extend to the other LLC members. In a two-member LLC, for example, one member is personally liable for his or her own negligent acts, but not for those of the other member.

> **EXAMPLE:** Otto, one of the two owners of Otto's Auto Parts Supply LLC, drives the LLC's Mazda Miata to pick up a throw-out bearing for a customer's Mercedes SUV. On the way, he negligently sideswipes a slow-moving Prius, a stunt that results in a $5,000 repair bill for damage to the Prius and a $25,000 medical claim for whiplash suffered by George, the Prius driver. If insurance doesn't cover George's damages, Otto can be held personally liable for the $30,000 (the LLC itself can be liable too if the accident happened on company time). But Mike, the other owner of the LLC, shouldn't be held personally liable for Otto's careless driving, nor should he be held personally liable if George obtains a legal judgment against the LLC itself.

Although LLC law does not protect members and managers from the consequence of their own torts, insurance can. Commercial, automotive, workers' compensation, or even the individual's homeowners' policy may cover some or all of the damage caused by an LLC manager's or member's tort. But don't rely on personal policies to provide business-related protection. It's essential to get a reasonable amount of appropriate liability insurance to cover potential personal and business liabilities arising from LLC operations. Typically, a commercial general liability insurance policy will cover the following:

- torts caused by business owners and employees in the course of business or on the business premises (a policy for bodily injury and property damage—so-called "slip-and-fall" coverage), and
- fire, theft, and a long list of catastrophes.

Of course, a general liability policy won't cover damages caused by a member's illegal or fraudulent behavior.

## Special Considerations for Professionals

If an LLC is organized to render licensed professional services such as health care, law, accounting, architecture, engineering, and similar services, state law normally renders each individual professional personally liable for his or her own malpractice, even if the business is organized as a corporation, LLC, PLLC (professional LLC), or RLLP (registered limited liability partnership—see Chapter 2). That's why it's essential for each person to purchase adequate malpractice insurance to cover this additional professional tort liability.

Professionals who are considering forming an LLC should also know that some states may not *specifically* protect a professional in a multi-member LLC from personal liability for the malpractice of other professionals in the firm, (this exposure for the malpractice of another professional is known as "vicarious liability"). However, other state LLC, PLLC, and RLLP statutes do offer protection from vicarious liability

## Breach of Duty to the LLC

In a co-owned LLC, the managers (either its members in the case of a member-managed LLC or its specially appointed managers in the case of a manager-managed LLC) have a legal obligation to manage the LLC in good faith and in the best interests of the LLC and its members. This is known as their "duty of care," and is similar to corporate directors' and officers' duty to their corporation. If a member or manager of an LLC violates this duty of care, he or she can be held personally liable for any money damages that result.

Although it sounds threatening, this duty of care is a fairly relaxed legal standard. Managers have been held to violate it only if they do something intentionally fraudulent, illegal, or so clearly wrongheaded that a fair-minded person would conclude they were taking a grossly negligent risk. LLC members and managers are not normally personally responsible to the LLC or other members for honest mistakes or even poor judgment in the carrying out of their job-related duties.

LLC members and managers in smaller LLCs often rely primarily on commercial liability insurance to protect them from lawsuits brought by outsiders, at least at the onset. If they can afford to, they may decide to back up this basic coverage with personal liability policies covering members or nonmember managers for "insider" and other management-related lawsuits. Policies of this sort protect LLC members and managers from personal liability for their management decisions (these policies should be distinguished from commercial liability insurance policies, which insure the LLC against catastrophic damage and injuries to employees and outsiders).

The duty of care applies to managers' actions toward all members of the LLC. For example, in a manager-managed LLC, the nonmanaging LLC members can sue a manager who knowingly entered a fraudulent transaction that hurt the LLC financially. And in member-managed LLCs, a member who violates the duty of care might be personally liable in a lawsuit by the other members.

**EXAMPLE 1:** Fred is the sole manager of a real estate LLC. The LLC owns an apartment building, which Fred manages. Because of high tenant vacancies and extra repair costs, the LLC reports a loss for the year and is unable to distribute profits to its members at the end of the year. The nonmanaging members sue Fred for failing to properly manage the LLC. As long as Fred has done his best to obtain tenants and make reasonably necessary repairs, he should be able to show that he has met his duty of care—and, therefore, win the lawsuit.

**EXAMPLE 2:** Robert, Juliet, and Greg are the three owners of the Lucky Lock Company LLC, a member-managed LLC. They vote at a management meeting on whether to use one-quarter of the company's cash reserves to market and sell the Neon Big-Lock Clock, a unique, three-by-five-foot lock plate with a neon clock display, which Robert invented. Greg is against the idea of committing company funds to promote a device that he believes no one will buy. But Robert and Juliet disagree with Greg, believing that the big clock will find a market. The neon clock idea does not catch on and Lucky Lock goes broke. Greg sues Robert and Juliet in their personal capacity. The judge finds that, although they made what turned out to be a bad business decision, Robert and Juliet did so armed with all the facts and in good faith, and did not breach their duty of care.

But now let's change a few facts and assume Robert and Juliet have researched the availability of certain key parts and know that several would have to be custom-made, which means the Neon Big-Lock Clock will be very difficult and expensive to produce. Instead of telling Greg these facts, they keep their knowledge secret and vote to go ahead with the project. This time when Greg sues, the judge supports his claim and finds that Juliet and Robert have breached their duty of care. Greg is awarded a significant judgment.

Robert and Juliet were liable in the second situation because of the way courts have interpreted a business owner's duty of care. A company's management has to follow the "business judgment" rule to avoid liability. This rule says that in making management decisions, managers will not be personally liable for honest business mistakes. Decisions that have some rational basis (based on facts known to managers or reported to them by someone with superior knowledge) should not give rise to personal liability even if they turn out to be mistaken and result in financial loss to the business and its owners. Let's go back to the Lucky Lock Company and change the scenario one more time.

> **EXAMPLE 3:** Again, Robert, Juliet, and Greg discuss at a management meeting whether to use one-quarter of the company's cash reserves to market and sell the Neon Big-Lock Clock. This time, Robert and Juliet disclose to Greg that certain essential parts would be very difficult and expensive to produce. Based on this disclosure, Greg is even more against the idea of committing company funds to promote a device that he is strongly convinced will not appeal to many customers. Greg's opinion, along with the information that casts doubt on the profitability of the Neon Big-Lock Clock, is fully discussed at the membership meeting. Nevertheless, based on their experience in the clock business and the fact that many offbeat designs (for example, the cuckoo clock) have been extremely profitable, Robert and Juliet vote to proceed (and Greg is outvoted two to one).
>
> Again, the Neon Big-Lock Clock is a disaster. Can Greg successfully sue the other owners personally for their bad business judgment? No, according to the business judgment rule. Robert and Juliet made an informed business decision without under-handedness, concealment, misrepresentation of facts, or other fraud or illegality. The fact that they guessed wrong should not make them personally liable to Greg.

TIP

**Disclose, disclose, disclose!** The above example highlights a basic LLC management rule: Full and fair disclosure of all material facts is part and parcel of LLC managers' and members' duty of care to the LLC. As long as this duty is met, the business judgment rule will normally protect members and managers from personal liability for their management decisions.

If an LLC member or manager is sued for breaching his or her duty to the LLC, can't the costs of the suit alone be disastrous to the defending member or manager? Not necessarily. If the member or manager wins the lawsuit, the laws of many states permit or require "indemnification" by the LLC. This means that the LLC must pay any legal expenses, fines, fees, and other liabilities owed by the LLC member or manager. But again, state rules often require the person to be indemnified to have acted in good faith and in the best interests of the LLC to receive indemnification. And, as you might guess, intentional misconduct, fraud, and illegal acts normally aren't covered under these rules.

CAUTION

**Financially irresponsible acts can also lead to a loss of limited liability.** As I mentioned above, an LLC must satisfy certain financial standards before a managing member or a manager can approve a distribution of profits. These standards prohibit an LLC from paying out profits if it can't afford it. If these standards are ignored and the company is later sued, the member or manager who approved the distribution may be personally on the hook for the amount of the invalid distribution. See Chapter 4 for more on this.

## Losing Your Limited Liability

In the situations above, LLC members can be held personally liable for specific acts or events that occur in the course of their business. But the limited liability status of the LLC itself can also be lost, if a court finds that you didn't run the LLC as a separate business entity.

Because the LLC is a relatively new business form, state courts have not had much time to flesh out all the legal implications of doing business as an LLC. The result is that there are not a lot of court decisions dealing with the issue of when an LLC should be treated as a sham entity and its members held liable in their personal capacities.

On the other hand, state courts have had plenty of time to discuss and interpret the limited liability protection that *corporations* provide to their owners, and to carve out exceptions to a corporation's limited liability status under extreme circumstances. Most legal commentators believe that state courts will follow the guidelines set out in these corporate cases when the limited liability protection offered by an LLC is challenged in state court. Because I agree that this is likely to happen, it makes sense to briefly look at instances where courts are likely to disregard a corporation's separate legal status and hold its owners personally liable (in legal slang, "pierce the corporate veil").

Generally, corporate limited liability protection will be disregarded—that is, the corporate owners will be held personally liable for business debts and claims—only in extreme cases. Typically, this occurs when owners fail to respect the separate legal existence of their corporation, but instead treat it as an extension of their personal affairs. For example, if owners fail to follow routine corporate formalities, such as adequately investing in or capitalizing the corporation, issuing stock, holding meetings of directors and shareholders, and keeping business records and transactions separate from those of the owners, a court is likely to find that the corporation doesn't really exist and that its owners are really doing business as individuals who are personally liable for their acts.

What does all of this mean for an LLC? Well, for starters, because many states' statutes specifically allow LLCs to act more informally than corporations (for example, they don't have to hold regular meetings), the failure to adhere to corporate formalities should not be a problem. But you should follow these basic precautions:

- **Act fairly and legally.** Do not conceal or misrepresent material facts or the state of your finances to vendors, creditors, or other outsiders. Or put more bluntly, don't engage in fraud.

- **Fund your LLC adequately.** You don't have to invest a lot of money in your LLC, but do try to put enough cash or other liquid assets in at the beginning so your LLC will be able to meet foreseeable expenses and liabilities. If you fail to do this, it is possible that a court faced with a balance sheet that shows a very minimal investment may disregard your LLC's limited liability protection. This is particularly likely if you engage in a risky business that obviously requires a substantial operating budget.

- **Keep LLC and personal business separate.** Nothing will encourage a court to disrespect your LLC entity more than your own failure to respect its status as an entity separate from its owners. This means you'll want to open up a separate LLC business bank account. As a routine business practice, write all checks for LLC expenses or payouts of profits out of this account, and deposit all LLC revenue into it. Do all of this even if you set up a single-member LLC. And of course, you will want to keep separate accounting books for your LLC—these can consist of a simple single-entry system, such as your LLC check register and deposit slips, but a double-entry system will serve you better when it comes time to prepare your end-of-year income tax returns, especially if yours is a multi-member company, which will have to prepare and file IRS Form 1065, the informational return for partnerships (see Chapter 4). You should also keep written records of all major LLC decisions.

## When Personal Creditors Can Go After LLC Assets

As explained above, the LLC's limited liability shield protects the personal assets of LLC owners from lawsuits that arise from LLC business operations and claims, with a few exceptions. However, this protection doesn't always work the other way—that is, an LLC owner's business assets are not necessarily protected from creditors seeking to satisfy personal debts or lawsuit judgments against the owner.

In most states, a personal creditor of an LLC owner can seize the owner's interest in the LLC. Because an interest in an LLC is the personal property of each LLC owner, personal creditors are typically allowed to obtain a "charging order" against the owner's interest in a business, such as a partnership interest, an LLC interest, or stock in a corporation. Essentially, a charging order is a lien against the owner's business interest, which allows the creditor to receive profit payments that would otherwise go to the owner.

> EXAMPLE: Sam defaults on a personal bank loan unrelated to his LLC business, and the bank obtains a charging order against Sam's LLC membership interest. This order allows the bank to be paid any profits that would otherwise be distributed to Sam under the terms of the LLC's operating agreement.

A charging order may not do a creditor much good if an LLC does not regularly distribute profits to members. In that case, the creditor may be able to ask a state court to foreclose on the LLC member's interest. If state law allows this and the court agrees, the creditor can become the new legal owner of the LLC. However, under most state laws, a creditor who forecloses on an LLC interest does not become a full owner. Instead, the foreclosing creditor becomes a "transferee" or "assignee" who is entitled to all economic rights associated with the interest, such as a share of the profits paid out on the interest and the value of the interest when the business is sold or liquidated. Typically, an assignee or transferee cannot manage or vote in the LLC, nor assume other membership rights granted to full members under the LLC operating agreement. Again, if the LLC does not pay out profits regularly and there is little chance of the business being sold or liquidated, these economic rights might not mean much to a creditor.

> CAUTION
>
> **Exception in some states for one-owner LLCs.** In a small number of states, if a court orders the foreclosure of a member's interest in a single-member LLC, the person who buys the foreclosed interest becomes a full member with voting rights. Even worse (for the original owner), in one of these exceptional states, the old owner has to go, and the new owner (the one who bought the interest in the court-approved sale of the original owner's interest), becomes the new owner of the LLC.

Some states allow transferees or assignees of LLC memberships to petition a court to force a dissolution of the LLC. This is an extreme remedy that may be available to creditors who can foreclose on an LLC membership interest in some states. To determine whether an LLC owner's personal creditor can obtain a charging order, foreclose, and/or force a dissolution of your LLC, consult a knowledgeable business lawyer.

**RESOURCE**

**State-by-state information on charging orders and foreclosure for single-member LLCs.** For more information on state laws on charging orders and foreclosures, visit to Nolo's overview of state laws on the subject at www.nolo.com/llc-foreclosure.

## Basics of Forming an LLC

In Chapter 6 I discuss in detail what you'll need to do to form an LLC. This section covers the basic requirements.

### What Types of Businesses Can Form LLCs?

With few exceptions, LLCs may be formed for all types of businesses. You may even form one LLC to engage in several businesses—for example, furniture sales, trucking, and redecorating can all be operated under one legal (if not physical) roof. But certain kinds of businesses, mostly financial in nature, may either be restricted or prohibited from setting up an LLC in your state. For example, companies that engage in the banking, trust, or insurance business are typically prohibited from forming LLCs.

Certain professionals may also be prohibited from forming an LLC in some states, or at least be subject to special rules when forming one. For example, the initial LLC members may need to obtain a statement from their state licensing board, certifying that they all have current state licenses, and file it with their LLC articles. State restrictions for professionals apply to doctors and other licensed health care workers, lawyers, accountants and, in some states, other professionals such as engineers and architects. In some states, such as California, certain professionals are not able to form an LLC and may need to form a professional corporation or partnership (RLLP) instead. In other states, professionals may have to form a PLLC (professional LLC) or at least follow special procedures if they choose to form an LLC. Typically, they must comply with one or more of the following rules:

- Only licensed professionals in a single profession—or in a group of related professions—may own a membership interest in a professional LLC.
- A PLLC must use a special LLC designator in its name— typically the words "Professional Limited Liability Company" or the abbreviation "PLLC."
- Each member must carry a specified amount of malpractice insurance.

 CAUTION

**Call your state LLC filing office if you are a licensed professional.** If you have a vocational or professional license, before spending any more time reading about LLCs, you should call your state LLC filing office to see if you can form an LLC in your state. Also ask about any special rules or restrictions. You may have to (or be able to) form a PLLC, professional corporation, or an RLLP instead. An experienced business lawyer in your state can help you choose the best structure for your professional practice.

## State LLC Laws

LLCs are regulated by the statutes (laws) of the state where they are formed. Each state, plus the District of Columbia, has an LLC act in place. And, because state legislators are not beyond a little legal plagiarism, it is common to see a remarkable degree of similarity between one state's LLC act and the acts of nearby states.

Although state LLC statutes do not make for the most scintillating reading, there are many instances when you can save yourself a bundle in legal fees by doing your own LLC research. For example, you may want your LLC operating agreement to include procedures for buying out the membership interest of a departing member. While state LLC law usually gives you great latitude in drafting your LLC operating agreement, this is one area where states may have mandatory requirements. Some states require the LLC to pay a departing member the fair value of the membership interest within a reasonable time after his or her departure. The statute may also say what the minimum fair value of the interest can be, or how it must be determined, or the maximum time a departing member must wait to receive payment.

## Model LLC Acts

Efforts have been made toward standardizing LLC laws, including the drafting of the Revised Prototype Limited Liability Company Act, sponsored by the American Bar Association's Section of Business Law, and the Revised Uniform Limited Liability Company Act, developed by the National Conference of Commissioners on Uniform State Laws. A growing number of states have adopted some or all of the provisions of these model acts into their state statutes. However, significant differences can exist among the laws in these states, so make sure to look up the law in your state if you wish to track a specific LLC Act provision.

LLC statutes are generally not lengthy. In just a few minutes, you should be able to find the section of law you are interested in. In Chapter 7, I discuss how to find and research your state's statutes. Of course, once you have read the statutes yourself, it makes sense to check your conclusions with a lawyer. But this should cost less than it would if you relied on the lawyer to do the basic statutory research and explain what the law says.

## How to Form an LLC

The basic legal step required to create an LLC in most states is to prepare and file LLC "articles of organization" with your state's LLC filing office. (Some states call this document a "certificate of organization" or a "certificate of formation.") Many states supply a blank one-page form for the articles of organization—you'll simply need to fill it out and send it in with a filing fee.

Some states allow you to prepare and file LLC articles online, from the secretary of state's website. (See Appendix A for contact information.) Typically, you need only specify a few basic details about your LLC, such as its name, principal office address, agent, and office for receiving legal papers, and the names of its initial members (or managers, if you're designating a special management team to run the LLC). I'll discuss articles of organization in more detail in Chapter 6.

One disadvantage to forming an LLC rather than a partnership or sole proprietorship is that you'll have to pay a filing fee when you file your articles to create your LLC. But in most states, the fees are modest (although the states of Massachusetts, Illinois, and Texas, among a few others, sock it to new LLCs). Also, this filing fee is a one-time-only fee in most states. For most LLC owners, it's a small price to pay for the peace of mind they get by having limited liability. Some states do, however, have larger recurring annual fees, which range from $100 to $500 each year. California, for example, charges an annual minimum franchise tax of $800, plus an additional "total income" fee (calculated on gross income plus the cost of goods sold, paid, or incurred in connection with the trade or business) that can reach up to $12,000 per year for high-income LLCs.

A few states (including New York) require you to take an additional step before your LLC will be official: in a local newspaper, you must publish a simple notice of your intent to form an LLC.

Once your articles of organization are on file and any publication requirement is met, your LLC is "official." But even though it is not required by state law, you also should create an LLC operating agreement. This is the document where you set out the ownership rules for your business (much like a partnership agreement or the bylaws of a corporation). A typical operating agreement includes:

- the members' capital interests
- the rights and responsibilities of members
- how profits and losses will be allocated
- how the LLC will be managed
- the voting power of all the members (and any managers)
- rules for holding meetings and taking votes, and
- buyout provisions, which lay down a framework for what happens when a member wants to sell his or her interest, dies, or becomes disabled.

You should have an operating agreement even if your LLC has just one or two members. The main reason is as simple as it is important. An operating agreement makes it more likely that a state court will respect the LLC's limited personal liability protection for its owners. This is particularly key in a one-person LLC, which—without the formality of an agreement—looks a lot like a sole proprietorship. Once your paperwork is completed and filed, you're ready to do business! See the checklist for forming an LLC in Appendix C for some more practical details.

**RESOURCE**

**Practical information on starting and running a business.** Nolo offers many helpful resources that explain the steps involved in opening any new business. First, check out Nolo's website at www.nolo.com. Here you'll find articles and FAQs full of free tips for starting your business. For more, read Nolo's best-selling book *Legal Guide for Starting & Running a Small Business*, by Fred S. Steingold. It offers a comprehensive, two-volume treatment for entrepreneurs on how to start and operate a business. *The Small Business Start-Up Kit: A Step-by-Step Legal Guide*, by Peri H. Pakroo, gives you a quick lowdown on how to open the doors of your new business quickly, from choosing a name, to finding a location, getting a business license, and much more.

# The LLC vs. Other Business Structures

To decide whether the LLC structure makes sense for your business, you must understand the other options. After all, your larger goal is to decide which type of business ownership structure ("business entity," in legal jargon) is right for you. I've already said that the LLC mixes and matches a number of the best attributes of other business forms. Now it's time for me to back up this assertion.

## Other Business Structures

There are three traditional ways of doing business:

- sole proprietorships
- partnerships, and
- C (regular) corporations.

There are two variants of these traditional business forms that are somewhat similar to an LLC:

- limited partnerships, and
- S corporations.

And just to make matters more complicated, all 50 states have also recently added another type of business entity that's even newer than the LLC. It's called the registered limited liability partnership (RLLP), sometimes simply called an LLP (limited liability partnership).

Let's briefly look at each of these business structures.

## What Is a Sole Proprietorship?

The simplest way of being in business for yourself is as a "sole proprietor." This is just a fancy way of saying that you are the owner of a one-person business. There's almost no cost or bureaucratic red tape required to form a sole proprietorship, other than getting a business license, perhaps applying for a sales tax permit, and following the local and state regulations that any business must face. As a practical matter, most one-person businesses start out as sole proprietorships just to keep things simple.

EXAMPLE: Remember Winston, the graphic artist we introduced at the beginning of this book who started moonlighting in his own home-based computer graphics business? Because Winston works in his business part time and has no employees, just a couple of clients, and no pressing personal liability issues, he chooses to operate as a sole proprietor. Outside of getting a business license, filing to use a fictitious name, and perhaps getting a tax permit (which any new business might have to do), Winston does not need to file any legal paperwork. Like all other one-person business owners, unless Winston takes steps to change the legal structure of his business—such as forming a one-person LLC or corporation—his one-person business will be automatically classified and treated as a sole proprietorship by the IRS and state.

## Number of Owners

By definition, a sole proprietorship has only one owner. If your one-person business grows and you wish to include other owners, you will need to move to a more complicated type of business structure. The minute you begin to own and split profits with another person, you automatically have a partnership on your hands. Or, you can choose instead to form an LLC or a corporation by filing papers with the state.

## Personal Liability for Business Debts

Unfortunately, although a sole proprietorship is legally very simple, it can also be a risky way to operate. As explained in Chapter 1, the sole proprietor is 100% personally liable for all business debts and legal claims. For example, if someone slips and falls in a sole proprietor's business and sues, the owner is responsible for paying any resulting court award (unless commercial liability insurance covers it). Similarly, if the business fails to pay suppliers, banks, or other bills, the owner is personally liable for the unpaid debts. This means the owner's personal assets, such as his or her bank accounts, equity in a house or car, and

## If You Own a Business With Your Spouse

Generally, an unincorporated business run by a husband and wife who share in its profits and losses is considered a partnership, not a sole proprietorship. There are a few exceptions to these general rules, however, which allow businesses owned by spouses to be treated as sole proprietorships:

- If one spouse manages the business and the other helps out as an employee or volunteer worker (but does not help run the business), the managing spouse can claim ownership and treat the business as a sole proprietorship.
- If (1) the business is not a corporation or other business entity (such as an LLC or limited partnership), (2) the only members of the business are a husband and wife who file a joint tax return, (3) both spouses materially participate in the business, and (4) both spouses elect not to be treated as a partnership (that is, the spouses do not file a separate partnership return for the business), then the spouses can divide the business profits and report them separately on their joint tax return. They do this by filing two Schedule Cs with their joint tax return (one for each spouse), showing each spouse's share of profits. Both spouses also must file a self-employment tax schedule (Schedule SE) to pay self-employment tax on their individual share of the profits. Each spouse gets Social Security credit for his or her share of earnings in the business.
- An unincorporated business that is owned solely by a husband and wife in the community property states of Arizona, California, Idaho, Louisiana, Nevada, New Mexico, Texas, Washington, and Wisconsin can treat itself as a sole proprietorship. The couple must file an IRS Form 1040 Schedule C for the business, listing one of the spouses as the owner. Only the listed spouse pays income and self-employment taxes on the business profits. This means only the spouse listed as owner will receive Social Security account earning credits for the Form SE taxes paid (this is why some eligible spouses decide not to make this Schedule C filing and continue to file a partnership tax return). There may be tax consequences for filing a Schedule C, as well.

For more information on spousal businesses, see IRS Publication 541, *Partnerships* (particularly the section on forming a partnership) and other information on the IRS website, www.irs.gov. Also, be sure to check with your tax adviser before deciding on the best way to own, and file and pay taxes for, a spousal business.

other personal property can be grabbed (attached) and sold to provide funds to repay business debts and judgments.

Of course, some businesses are much more vulnerable to debts and lawsuits than others. If yours is a small, part-time business that does not operate on credit and is highly unlikely to face a lawsuit, you needn't lie awake worrying about these issues.

## Paying Taxes

A sole proprietor reports business profits or losses on IRS Schedule C, *Profit or Loss From Business (Sole Proprietorship)*, filed with his or her federal tax return. The owner's profits are taxed at his or her individual income tax rates. This is called "pass-through" taxation because the income passes through the business to the owner's individual tax return. In other words, like a partnership, a sole proprietorship is not a separate taxable "business entity" under the federal tax scheme. Instead, the tax law says a sole proprietorship is "disregarded as an entity separate from its owner."

Most startup business owners prefer pass-through taxation of their business income, at least in the beginning. Why? Reporting and paying individual income taxes by preparing a Schedule C (and a Schedule SE for self-employment tax) is a lot less complicated than preparing a partnership or corporate return. In fact, many small business owners can do the Schedule C and Schedule SE work themselves.

Because a sole proprietor is self-employed, it might seem that his or her business income will be subject to an increased self-employment (Social Security and Medicare) tax rate—about twice the rate a corporate employee would personally pay. In fact, the actual amount of self-employment taxes that a sole proprietor pays turns out to be the same as what he or she would pay if the business was organized as a one-person corporation and taxed separately. That's because the owner-employee of a corporation personally pays half of his or her Social Security and Medicare taxes, and the corporation pays the other half, whereas the sole proprietor simply pays the total amount in one lump sum, as self-employment tax.

## Sole Proprietorships Compared to LLCs

As mentioned, no organizational fees or paperwork are required to start a sole proprietorship. By contrast, forming an LLC requires you to pay some state filing fees (see Chapter 1 for a discussion of state filing fees). Starting an LLC also requires you to complete organizational papers, including articles of organization and an operating agreement. Operating an LLC may require more ongoing record keeping than running a sole proprietorship. To make sure your LLC operates efficiently, you'll want to keep written records of all major LLC decisions. In addition, all LLC financial transactions should be kept on the LLC books, separate from the finances of the LLC owners. You'll need to set up a separate LLC bank account, making sure to pay all expenses and payouts of profits from this account. Separating the LLC's finances like this will help show a court (if necessary) that your business really is a distinct legal entity.

This extra work and money is the trade-off you make in exchange for the LLC's biggest advantage: personal liability protection for its owners. While a commercial insurance policy can lessen a sole proprietor's liability for business mistakes and accidents, most affordable commercial policies contain high deductibles, meaning that even if it's available, most smaller businesses can't afford to buy full coverage for all foreseeable risks. And, of course, no insurance policy will protect owners from their failure to pay ordinary debts of the business, such as money owed to banks, landlords, suppliers, and other creditors. LLC owners, on the other hand, are protected from these liabilities as long as the owners do not agree to be personally liable for the business's debts (for example, by cosigning for business loans).

Keep in mind that, as your business grows and becomes more profitable, so too does your exposure to lawsuits. Increased profits are invariably tied to increased business activity—for example, more customer transactions—and this means more potential for getting sued. And, of course, the very fact that your business is making more money often means that you look like a better target for attorneys who, it's sad to say, often decide to sue the "deepest pockets" they can find when a dispute or accident happens.

**EXAMPLE:** Rita and Ron move to Kona, Hawaii, buy a six-seat outboard-motor Zodiac boat, and start earning a little cash giving whale-watching tours with their new business, Kona Coast Roamer Tours. In the early days business is slow, and the two partners alternate taking out clients for a couple of hours a few times each week. But as the mainland economy booms and tourists flock to Hawaii, their business blooms too. In fact, it improves so much the duo buy two additional boats and hire two staff members to provide morning and afternoon tours, seven days a week. This increased activity makes Ron and Rita nervous— more tours mean the potential for more accidents and personal liability exposure for the owners. This nervousness increases more than a little when Rita discovers she's pregnant and the couple decide to buy a house. To help restore calm, Ron and Rita decide to form an LLC to get its personal limited liability protection, and to sleep a little better at night. This is, after all, why they moved to Hawaii in the first place.

When it comes to tax costs, sole proprietorships and LLCs come out about even on the main tax issues:

- **Income taxes.** Sole proprietorships and LLCs are both automatically treated as pass-through tax entities. Therefore, sole proprietors and one-person LLC owners can count on about the same amount of tax complexity, paperwork, and costs. Of course, if a one-person LLC elects corporate tax treatment (see Chapter 4), the LLC's tax situation will change significantly, to mirror that of a corporation. And co-owned LLCs must file an informational partnership tax return.
- **Self-employment taxes.** Both sole proprietors and the sole owners of one-person LLCs will likely have the same self-employment tax burden. (See Chapter 4 for a discussion of self-employment taxes for LLC members.)

# What Is a General Partnership?

A partnership is a business in which two or more owners agree to share profits (and losses). If you go into business with at least one other person, state law says you have automatically formed a general partnership, even if you never sign a formal partnership agreement. A general partnership really can be started with a handshake, although it makes far more sense to prepare and sign a written partnership agreement, as explained below.

> EXAMPLE: Two employed Web designers set up a side business to design websites for nonprofit organizations. They are too busy working to bother thinking about the best business structure for their new sideline business. Without taking any formal action or creating a partnership agreement, they have formed a partnership. If the partners were to have a dispute—over the division of profits perhaps—state partnership law would determine how it had to be resolved, unless the partners had a written agreement covering the issue. This is one good reason why taking the time to prepare a partnership agreement in this sort of co-owned business is so important. For now, working as partners suits these two Web designers, because there are no significant personal liability issues involved in operating their tiny business. If their business grows, and along with it their business debt, they might consider forming an LLC.

 TIP

**All partnerships should create a written partnership agreement.**
While not required by law, general partners should always create a written partnership agreement. Without an agreement, the one-size-fits-all rules of each state's general partnership laws will apply to the partnership. These provisions usually say that profits and losses of the business should be divided up equally among the partners (or according to the partner's capital contributions in some states), and they impose a long list of other cookie-cutter rules. Rather than relying on state law, general partners should prepare a written partnership

agreement (much like an LLC operating agreement) that covers issues important to their business relationship, including division of profits and losses, partnership draws (guaranteed payments to partners), and the procedure for selling a partnership interest back to the partnership or to an outsider, should a partner die or want to move on.

## Number of Partners

General partnerships may be formed by two or more people; by definition, there is no such thing as a one-person partnership. Legally, there is no upper limit on the number of partners who may be admitted into a partnership, but, because partnerships lack the organizational and management structure that is built into corporations and LLCs, partnerships with many owners may have problems reaching a consensus on business decisions and may be subject to divisive disputes between contending management factions. In larger partnerships, one or more partners may be designated as managing partners to eliminate day-to-day bickering, but using a partnership agreement to delegate authority to a select group of managing partners is rare in small business partnerships. Why? Because doing so can be risky for the nonmanaging partners—who, by definition, wouldn't keep a close eye on the business. Remember, all general partners are personally liable for partnership debts, whether they show up for work every day or not. To minimize their risks and to keep their partners honest, all general partners usually take an active hand in management.

## Personal Liability for Business Debts

Each owner of a general partnership is personally liable for all business debts and any claims (including court judgments) against the business that the business can't pay. For example, if the business fails to pay its suppliers, the partners are personally responsible for paying these business debts and may have to use their houses, cars, and personal bank accounts to come up with the money.

What's more, if the business owes money It can't pay, the creditor may go after any general partner for the entire debt, regardless of the partner's ownership percentage (although if this happens, the partner who is sued can in turn sue the other partners to force them to repay their shares of the debt).

Personal liability for business debts is even more worrisome because each general partner may bind the entire partnership (and all of its partners) to a contract or business deal. In legal jargon, this authority is expressed by saying that each partner is an *agent* of the partnership. (Fortunately, there are a few significant limitations to this agency rule— to be valid, a contract or deal must generally be within the scope of the partnership's business, and the outside person who makes the deal with a partner must reasonably think that the partner is authorized to act on behalf of the partnership.) If a partnership can't fulfill a valid contract or other business deal, each partner may be held personally liable for the amount owed. This personal liability for the debts of the entire partnership, coupled with the agency authority of each partner to bind the others, makes the general partnership riskier than a sole proprietorship and far riskier than LLCs, corporations, limited partnerships, and RLLPs (all of which offer at least some of the owners limited personal liability for business debts).

## Paying Taxes

Like a sole proprietorship, a general partnership is a pass-through tax entity. Again, this means profits (and losses) pass through the business entity to the partners, who pay taxes on any profits on their individual returns at their individual tax rates.

Partnership taxation, however, is a lot more complicated than sole proprietorship taxation, and most partnerships of any size will likely need an accountant. Although a partnership does not pay its own taxes, it must file an informational return each year, IRS Form 1065, *U.S. Return of Partnership Income*. In addition, the partnership must give each partner a filled-in IRS Schedule K-1 (Form 1065), *Partner's Share of Income, Deductions, Credits, etc.,* which shows the share of profits or losses each partner carries over to his or her individual 1040 tax return at the end of the year. Just like LLC members, each partner must pay taxes on his or her entire share of profits, even if the partnership chooses to reinvest the profits in the business rather than distributing them to the partners. The technical way of saying this is that the owners are taxed on their "allocated" profits, not their "distributed" profits. (I discuss this in the LLC context in Chapter 4.)

What about self-employment (Social Security and Medicare) taxes? General partners must pay self-employment taxes on their share of partnership income.

## General Partnerships Compared to LLCs

General partnerships are less costly to start than LLCs because most states do not require partnerships to file start-up paperwork with a state agency, so there are no filing fees for forming new general partnerships (although some states require partnerships to publish a notice in a local newspaper). By contrast, an LLC will have to file organizational papers and pay state filing fees. Also, operating a co-owned LLC often requires more ongoing record keeping than running a partnership—it's wise to record LLC management decisions to avoid disputes among LLC owners and to show, if necessary, that you're treating the LLC as a separate business entity. Partnerships, too, should try to keep written records of key business and ownership decisions, but there are fewer potential legal consequences if they fail to do so.

The big downside to running a general partnership is each partner's exposure to personal liability. A general commercial insurance package, possibly supplemented by more specialized coverage for particular risks, can significantly lessen the partners' exposure to personal liability for accidents. However, most affordable commercial insurance policies contain high deductibles and do not cover certain transactions, such as mismanagement or risky behavior by the business owners, and most smaller businesses can't afford to buy full coverage for all foreseeable risks.

In addition, no insurance policy will cover the failure to pay ordinary debts of the business, such as money owed to banks, landlords, and other creditors. LLC owners, on the other hand, are not personally liable for these debts.

General partnerships and LLCs come out about even on a couple of important issues:

- **Ownership agreements.** Even a small general partnership should start off with a written general partnership agreement. Creating one, of course, takes time and, if a lawyer is hired to write it, is likely to cost between $1,000 and $5,000 in legal fees, depending on the complexity of your partnership. Of course, many partners do the work themselves using a self-help resource. Creating a partnership agreement with one of these tools takes about as much time as it takes to create an LLC operating agreement on your own.

- **Income taxes.** General partnerships and co-owned LLCs are both automatically treated as pass-through tax entities, and both prepare and file standard partnership tax returns. (There are no separate LLC tax returns at the federal level; co-owned LLCs are treated as partnerships for tax purposes and use the same informational tax returns and tax procedures as partnerships.) Therefore, partnership and LLC owners can count on about the same amount of tax complexity, paperwork, and costs. Even though you'll probably turn over most year-end tax work to a tax adviser who'll prepare your business tax return, understanding and following basic business reporting tax procedures takes a fair amount of time and effort for either type of business. Of course, both LLCs and partnerships can elect corporate tax treatment, which makes things more complicated (see Chapter 4).

As for self-employment taxes, general partners and LLC members usually pay self-employment taxes on their share of profits. (See Chapter 4 for a full discussion of self-employment taxes for LLC members.)

**RESOURCE**

**Start-up information for partnerships.** If you're considering forming a partnership rather than an LLC, Nolo offers several helpful resources for learning about partnerships and creating a partnership agreement. Nolo's website, www. nolo.com, offers free articles and FAQs about starting a partnership. In addition, Nolo's *Form a Partnership: The Complete Legal Guide*, by Denis Clifford and Ralph Warner, explains how to form a partnership and create a partnership agreement.

## What Is a Limited Partnership?

A limited partnership is similar to a general partnership, except it has two types of partners. A limited partnership must have at least one general partner who manages the business and is personally liable for its debts and claims. General partners have the same broad rights and responsibilities as the partners discussed in the general partnership section above.

A limited partnership must also have at least one limited partner, and usually has more. A limited partner is typically an investor who contributes capital to the business, but is not involved in day-to-day management. As long as limited partners do not participate in management, they do not have personal liability for business debts and claims. Instead, they function much like passive shareholders in a small corporation, investing with the expectation of receiving a share of both profits and the eventual increase in the value of the business.

To create a limited partnership, you must pay an initial fee and file papers with the state—usually a "certificate of limited partnership." This document is similar to the articles (or certificate) filed by a corporation or an LLC, and includes information about the general and limited partners. Filing fees are about the same for limited partnerships as for a corporation or an LLC.

As for income taxes, limited partnerships generally are treated like general partnerships, with all partners individually reporting and paying taxes on their share of the profits each year. The limited partnership files an informational partnership tax return (IRS Form 1065, *U.S. Return of Partnership Income*, the same tax form that applies to a general partnership or co-owned LLC), and each partner receives IRS Schedule K-1 (1065), *Partner's Share of Income, Deductions, Credits, etc.* from the partnership. Each partner then files this form with his or her individual tax return. Limited partners, as a rule, don't have to pay self-employment taxes. Because they are not active in the business, their share of partnership income is not considered "earned income" for purposes of self-employment taxes.

Limited partnerships and LLCs look alike in many ways. Both provide the limited liability owners with protection against business debts and claims, and both are treated as pass-through tax entities under the default tax rules. But there are two major differences. First, a limited partnership must have at least one general partner, who is personally liable for the debts and other liabilities of the business (unless the general partner goes to the trouble of setting up his or her own corporation or LLC, which I discuss below). This differs from LLCs, where all members are automatically covered by the cloak of limited liability protection.

Second, limited partners are generally prohibited from managing the business. A limited partner who becomes active in the business of the limited partnership typically loses his or her limited liability. Some states have carved out some new exceptions to this ban, however, usually allowing a limited partner to vote on issues that affect the basic structure of the partnership, including the removal of general partners, the termination of the partnership, the amendment of the partnership agreement, or the sale of all or most of the assets of the partnership. In contrast, all LLC members can manage and participate in any aspect of the business without running the risk of losing their limited liability.

This second restriction of the limited partnership makes it an unsuitable ownership form for many small, actively run businesses. If all or most owners will want to participate in decision making, this would subject them to personal liability for business debts in a limited partnership. If an owner of a limited partnership wants the benefit of limited liability protection, he or she must step back from active management and play the role of passive investor only—something that is all but impossible for most small business owners, who plan to be active in their own businesses. Owners who want to be active in their company are better off forming an LLC or a corporation, where all owners/investors can run the business while enjoying the protection of limited liability for business debts.

Although a limited partnership is far less versatile than an LLC, some companies still operate as limited partnerships. This usually happens in certain types of investment firms, where the investors insist that the managers of the company (the general partners) be on the hook for bad business decisions, thinking that the managers will be less likely to make unsound investments if their personal assets are at stake. But in other, usually larger, limited partnerships, the general partner is actually a limited liability enterprise such as an LLC or a corporation. This way, the general partner avoids personal liability too.

> **EXAMPLE:** In 1985, Situs Holdings, a limited partnership, was established as a real estate development company. Its general partner is The Situs Corporation, and it has 20 limited partners. The limited partners are people who invest capital to purchase and improve the company's real estate holdings, while the general partner, The Situs Corporation, manages Situs Holdings' properties in exchange for a management fee. The Situs Corporation is owned by Sid Block and his two daughters, Elizabeth and Jackie. All of the partners—The Situs Corporation and the limited partners—share in a percentage of the profits of Situs Holdings.
>
> Note that the general partner is a corporation. This is a standard technique used to limit the personal liability of the general partner in larger limited partnerships, particularly where the liabilities of the company may be hefty. In this situation, the company's real estate debts are substantial, and the potential liabilities associated with the renovation and sale of properties also are considerable— general contractor liability claims, purchaser rescissions, and other disputes that may run into the millions of dollars. Of course, the whole Situs ownership scheme was established before the LLC came into existence. If Sid and his daughters and the limited partners had to do it all over again, their legal and tax advisers would probably recommend a much simpler setup—namely,

forming one manager-managed LLC to hold and develop the properties. All of the LLC managers and the nonmanaging members (the investors) would enjoy limited liability protection.

# What Is a C Corporation?

A "C" corporation is just another name for a regular for-profit corporation —a corporation taxed under normal corporate income tax rules. The letter C comes from Subchapter C of the Internal Revenue Code and is used to distinguish regular corporations from "S" corporations, which are regulated under Subchapter S of the Internal Revenue Code. In a nutshell, an S corporation gets the pass-through tax treatment of a partnership (with some important technical differences) and the limited liability of a corporation, much like an LLC. I discuss S corporations in more detail below.

To form a corporation, you pay corporate filing fees and prepare and file formal organizational papers, usually called "articles of incorporation," with a state agency (in most states, the secretary or department of state). Once formed, the corporation assumes an independent legal life separate from its owners. This separate legal life leads to a number of familiar traditional corporate characteristics, which I discuss below.

## Number of Shareholders (Owners)

A corporation can have as many or as few shareholders as it wants. Most states allow one-person corporations, in which the sole owner and shareholder also fills any required director and officer slots.

## Limited Liability for Shareholders

A corporation provides all of its owners—that is, its shareholders—with the benefits of limited personal liability protection. If a court judgment is entered against the corporation, or the corporation can't pay its bills, the shareholders stand to lose only the money that they've invested. Creditors cannot go after the personal assets of the shareholders.

Traditionally, the main reason why business owners formed corporations was to avoid personal exposure to business debts and claims. Of course, now that LLCs have entered the picture, small business owners can choose between the two if they are looking for limited liability protection. I compare the two entities below.

## Paying Taxes

To understand corporate taxation, you need to know how unincorporated businesses are taxed. In an unincorporated business, the owners pay individual income taxes on all net profits of the business, regardless of how much they actually receive each year. For example, assume that a partnership or an LLC has two owners and earns $100,000 in net profits. If the owners split profits equally, each must report and pay individual income taxes on $50,000 of business profits. This is true even if all of the profits are kept in the business checking account to meet upcoming business expenses rather than paid out to the owners.

Now, let's compare how net profits are paid out and taxed in a corporation. A corporation is a legal entity separate from its shareholders and files its own tax return, paying taxes on any profits left in the business. Shareholders who work for the corporation are employees, who receive a share of the profits as salaries for their work in the business. The corporation deducts these salaries as a business expense when it computes its net taxable income. But because the owners of a small corporation also manage the business as its directors, they have the luxury of deciding how much to pay themselves in salary. This allows the owners to decide how much of the profits will be taxed at the corporate level or paid out to them and taxed on their individual returns.

Two results follow from this: (1) corporate owners pay individual income taxes only on salary amounts they actually receive, not on all the net profits of the business, and (2) the corporation pays corporate taxes on the net profits actually retained in the business—that is, profits that remain after paying normal business expenses, including the salaries paid to the working owners. The corporate tax scheme taxes the business on profits actually retained in the corporation, while taxing the owners only on profits they actually receive. This type of income splitting between the company and the owners can lead to tax savings, at least for small corporations.

The corporation's owners file individual income tax returns and pay taxes, at their individual tax rates, on the salaries and any bonuses they receive. At the end of the year, the corporation files a corporate tax return, IRS Form 1120, *U.S. Corporation Income Tax Return*, and pays its own income taxes on the profits left in the company. Corporate tax rates are normally lower than shareholders' individual tax rates for the first $75,000 of income (currently 15% for the first $50,000, 25% for the next $25,000). This means that if the owners decide to retain profits in the business for expansion or other business needs, profits of up to $75,000 will be taxed at rates that are typically lower than the owners' individual tax rates, resulting in overall tax savings.

| Tax Rates on Taxable Corporate Income | |
|---|---|
| $0 to $50,000 | 15% |
| $50,001 to $75,000 | 25% |
| $75,001 to $100,000 | 34% |
| $100,001 to $335,000 | 39% |
| $335,001 to $10,000,000 | 34% |
| $10,000,001 to $15,000,000 | 35% |
| $15,000,001 to $18,333,333 | 38% |
| Over $18,333,333 | 35% |

*Note:* Personal service corporations are subject to a flat tax of 35% regardless of how much (or how little) they earn.

**EXAMPLE:** Justine and Janine are partners in Just Jams & Jellies, a specialty store selling gourmet canned preserves. Business has boomed and their net taxable income has reached a level where it is taxed at an individual tax rate of 35%. If the owners incorporate, they can leave $75,000 worth of profits in their business, which will be taxed at the lower corporate tax rates of 15% and 25%, saving overall tax dollars on business income.

For some small businesses, however, this corporate tax strategy—called income splitting—isn't useful, because their owners pay out all net profits to themselves at the end of each tax year.

EXAMPLE 1: Remember our friend Winston, who set up his own computer graphics company as a sideline to his day job? Like many other small service-business owners, he does not reinvest profits of his self-employment business, but happily deposits every last cent into his own personal checking account. Would corporate tax treatment benefit Winston? No. He does not have any reason to accumulate money in his business, so he would not benefit from lower corporate tax rates.

EXAMPLE 2: Linux and Colleen own and work part time for their own LLC, a retail sales business that employs one full-time worker, Vince. Linux and Colleen share in the LLC's profits as owners. Gross sales revenue of the business this year is expected to be $200,000. Cost of inventory will be $50,000, so net sales revenue is $150,000. Linux and Colleen annually pay Vince $50,000 in salary and their landlord $25,000 to rent their storefront property. Other normal business expenses total about $20,000 per year, with the result that net profits will be about $55,000. The partners need to pay out all of this money to themselves to help meet their own living expenses (past savings also help them pay their personal expenses as their business gets going). Again, as in the example above, income splitting is not a viable tax strategy for this small business.

But for other small businesses, even ones with modest net incomes, income splitting might make sense. Many small business owners are forced to retain net profits in their businesses to handle upcoming costs of doing business, such as buying inventory or paying employee salaries and other necessary and regular business expenses such as rent and insurance. Owners may have to retain net profits in the business even if they are not paying out as much of the profits to themselves as they would like. In these situations, paying the lower corporate tax rates on net income left in the business may result in tax savings.

EXAMPLE: Let's visit Linux and Colleen a few years from now and assume that their LLC has begun to make more money. For the past two years, their gross sales have averaged $500,000, and their cost of inventory sold has remained level at 25% of gross sales, or $125,000. Vince, the one full-time employee, and the owners have had to work harder to meet increased customer demand, giving up many of their weekends to the business. Vince's salary has increased to $75,000, but other expenses have stayed almost level at $60,000. Net partnership profits now average $240,000 per year, with each owner taking home a $120,000 share.

Linux and Colleen agree to look for a slightly more upscale storefront, hoping to sell more expensive items (with higher margins) to a more affluent clientele. They know that they'll have to come up with a chunk of cash to move into a new space, and they also expect to have to come up with additional funds to start stocking the higher-priced inventory. In addition, they discuss the possibility of hiring another full-time worker—if only to give themselves more weekend time away from the business. They realize they'll have to take a temporary cut in their share of paid-out profits to fund the move and expansion. Realizing they will need to begin retaining a substantial amount of profits in the business in order to accomplish these plans, they decide to elect corporate tax treatment so that the profits kept in the business will be taxed at lower corporate income tax rates.

Now for one last income tax item: When a corporation is sold or dissolved, both the shareholders and their corporation must pay taxes on any increased value (appreciation) of the corporation's assets. This means that any appreciation is taxed twice, once to the corporation and once to the shareholders. For businesses that regularly make investments, hold real estate, or buy other types of property that are likely to increase in value, this can be a big disadvantage. The rules here are complex, but you should know that incorporating could lead to tax consequences when you sell or dissolve your business. This is definitely one of the areas where you should seek expert tax advice.

## Corporate Management

Because a corporation has a separate legal existence from its owners, you must pay more attention to its legal care and feeding than you would for a sole proprietorship, a partnership, or an LLC.

As mentioned above, corporations are owned by shareholders and managed by a board of directors. This means the owners of a small corporation must periodically don different legal hats. As directors they must hold annual meetings required under state law. And they must keep minutes of meetings, prepare formal documentation—in the form of resolutions or written consents to corporate actions—of important decisions made during the life of the corporation, and keep a paper trail of all legal and financial dealings between the corporation and its shareholders.

To make corporate life even more complicated, the board of directors needs to appoint officers to supervise daily corporate business. State law usually requires corporations to have at least a president (CEO) and a secretary; in many states, a treasurer is required as well. Because a small corporation's shareholders act as both its board of directors and its officers, this consists of little more than handing out a few more titles to the same people.

> **EXAMPLE:** Tornado Air Conditioning Service, Inc., is owned and operated by Ted and his wife Valerie. They name themselves as the only two directors in the corporate articles they file with the state. At the first organizational meeting of the board, they appoint Valerie as both president and treasurer, and Ted as both corporate VP and secretary. They also approve the issuance of the corporation's initial shares to Ted and Valerie, its only two shareholders.

## Corporate Capital and Stock Structure

A corporation issues stock to its shareholders in exchange for capital invested in the business. This ownership structure remains unique in the world of business entities and leads to a few special benefits. For example, a corporation can parcel out ownership interests in the form of shares, which can be divided into classes, each with different rights to vote, receive dividends, participate in management, and receive cash if the business is liquidated.

Corporate stock is also a very useful way to fund employee stock option or bonus plans. In addition, it can be used to fund a buyout of another business or can be exchanged or converted into the shares of another corporation to effect a potentially tax-free merger or consolidation. And, of course, the corporate stock structure is almost essential if a business wants to raise money from the public in an initial public offering (IPO). Each state's corporation statutes flesh out the full potential of corporate stock ownership and provide a ready-made set of legal standards and procedures that are used throughout the banking, investment, and legal community to funnel private and public capital into corporate coffers.

## Employee Fringe Benefits

Even small corporations have the opportunity to offer fringe benefits, such as tax-deductible group term life insurance, medical reimbursement plans, and other special corporate employee perks. The owner-employees who receive these benefits generally don't have to pay tax on their individual tax returns for the value of these benefits.

## Corporations Compared to LLCs

A good way to compare the C corporation to the LLC is to revisit the corporate benefits discussed above to see whether an LLC could achieve similar results. You'll find that many, but not all, of the advantages associated with incorporation can also be achieved by forming an LLC. What's more, an LLC provides its owners with several unique benefits that they could not achieve by incorporating.

- **Limited liability for all owners.** Like corporate shareholders, all LLC owners are protected from personal liability for business debts and claims under state law. The limited liability provided by LLCs is just as strong as that provided by corporations.

- **Corporate formalities.** Corporations are similar to LLCs in the type of paperwork and fees necessary to get them started. Both must prepare and file organizational papers with the state and pay a filing fee. And it is essential that both adopt operating rules that set out the basic legal requirements for operating the business: Corporations adopt bylaws and LLCs adopt operating agreements. But when it comes to ongoing paperwork hassles, LLCs are easier to manage. Small LLCs can avoid a lot of the ongoing formalities required of corporations, such as holding and documenting formal meetings. Of course, LLC members still should take the time to document important legal, tax, and business decisions, and even hold and document the occasional important member meeting if only to make sure everyone's on the same page and to record everyone's mutual understanding. But this is a practical, not a legal, requirement. Corporations, on the other hand, typically must hold shareholders' and directors' meetings at least annually, whether they are really needed or not.

- **Corporate management.** LLCs are not required to have the three-tiered organizational structure of corporations: shareholders, directors, and officers. In an LLC, all you need are owners (members). Some LLCs choose to select some of the members to be managers, but most members of smaller LLCs usually choose to operate their LLC themselves, without a separate management team. Even if an LLC does appoint managers to handle the day-to-day business, living with the manager/member dichotomy can be a lot simpler than trying to juggle the management roles of corporate shareholder, director, and officer.

- **Corporate stock structure.** As mentioned above, the corporation's special stock structure remains a unique part of the corporate way of life. While LLCs can issue informal "membership units," these units don't have the same legal or financial standing that corporate shares do—most importantly, there is no standard system in place for public offerings of membership units. And, of course, LLCs don't issue stock, so there can be no stock options (LLC membership options are tricky and expensive to set up). For these reasons, the small minority of small businesses that want to issue options to employees or sell shares to venture capitalists will find that organizing as a corporation makes the most sense.
- **Tax treatment of profits and losses.** For the great majority of companies that will never need the stock structure of corporations, forming an LLC may be the best choice simply because an LLC can split profits and losses among owners as the owners choose. For example, even in an LLC owned equally by four people, profits and losses can be apportioned in unequal percentages (as long as special IRS rules are followed). By comparison, corporate capitalization is more straightlaced. Because of the stock ownership model set out in corporate statutes, corporate profits and losses must normally be allocated in proportion to stock ownership. While special classes of shares can be created to deviate somewhat from the standard corporate model, this involves creating a complex stock structure.

EXAMPLE: Manny and Linda present a business idea to Nate, who agrees to give them financial backing. Nate puts up the cash to get the business started, while Manny and Linda contribute their great idea and personal know-how. They form an LLC with each as a one-third owner, but Nate insists on getting 50% of any LLC profits until he is paid back his cash investment plus 10% annual interest. The LLC structure easily accommodates this arrangement—they simply set out these terms in their operating agreement.

If the three had instead formed a corporation, a more complicated ownership arrangement would be required to effect the uneven profit distribution. One approach would be to issue Nate a separate class of shares that alone participate in dividends. But this setup would not be optimal, because dividends can't be deducted from corporate income. Instead, they must be paid with after-tax profits of the company (and would be taxed a second time on Nate's individual tax return). Alternatively, they might decide to exclude Nate totally from stock ownership in the business and instead have him lend money to the corporation, issuing him an interest-bearing note. But this approach, too, would be problematic: It would deny Nate a capital stake in the enterprise money, so he wouldn't profit if the business was later sold for a great price. Disproportionate profit-sharing arrangements are allowable in an LLC, but they are not so easily implemented in the corporate context.

- **Corporate income tax treatment and income splitting.** Traditionally, what set the corporate form apart from other limited liability structures (like the LLC) was corporate tax treatment, and specifically, the ability to split income between the business and its owners. In years past, owners of an unincorporated business such as an LLC or a partnership had to legally convert their business into a corporation in order to be treated as a corporation for income tax purposes. That's no longer true. Today, if you find that your LLC or partnership regularly retains profits to meet its future needs instead of distributing these profits, you have the option of electing to be taxed as if you were incorporated. By doing this, you'll pay individual income taxes on only the amount of profits actually paid to you for working in your business and let the business pay its own taxes on retained profits, at reduced corporate income tax rates (at least for the first $75,000 of profits). The net result may be a substantial income tax savings for you and the other business owners. For example, if your individual tax bracket is 31%, you'll save approximately $10,000 in taxes on $75,000 of retained profits.

As a practical matter, of course, most new LLCs don't want corporate tax treatment until their owners are able to take home plenty of profits to cover their living expenses. Even then, they do so only if their tax adviser agrees that the income tax savings that can be achieved by splitting income between owners and the business entity itself are worth the trouble and collateral tax costs of electing corporate tax treatment. (To find out more about corporate tax splitting for LLCs, see Chapter 4.)

- **Double tax on dissolution or sale.** Unlike shareholders and their corporations, LLC members and their LLC are not subject to double taxation on appreciated business assets when the LLC is dissolved or sold.

- **Taxation of benefits.** As mentioned above, corporations can offer employees qualified fringe benefits and deduct the cost as a business expense. While some of these fringe benefits are available under federal and state tax rules to sole proprietors and owners of partnerships and LLCs, unincorporated business owners who receive nonqualified benefits may have to pay tax on their value (unless they have elected corporate tax treatment). However, before you decide this is a big corporate advantage, remember that many new businesses can't afford the cost of these expensive benefits for all of their employees. And often, employee benefits must be provided on a nondiscriminatory basis to all employees or none—not just to the owners of the corporation. In short, the cost of setting up and maintaining elaborate benefit programs for all of a corporation's employees may offset the tax advantages for the owners.

That's the short list of key corporation and LLC similarities and differences. For many business owners, incorporation makes sense only if the business needs to take advantage of the corporate stock structure to attract key employees and investment capital (including possibly raising public capital by making a public offering of shares). For businesses that never go public, or businesses that will go public many years from now, choosing to operate as an LLC rather than a corporation normally makes the most sense because of its simplicity and flexibility.

**RESOURCE**

**Start-up information for corporations.** If forming a corporation makes more sense for your business than forming an LLC, Nolo offers several helpful resources for learning about and forming corporations. Nolo's website, www.nolo.com, offers free articles and FAQs about starting a corporation. In addition, I have written a national book good for forming a corporation in any state: Nolo's *Incorporate Your Business: A Legal Guide to Forming a Corporation in Your State.*

# What Is an S Corporation?

An S corporation is a corporation that qualifies for special tax treatment under the Internal Revenue Code and state corporate tax statutes. Forming one entails the same paperwork requirements as forming a regular C corporation: filing articles of incorporation with the state and paying a state filing fee. Then, the shareholders have to convert the new corporation into an S corporation by signing and filing IRS Form 2553, *Election by a Small Business Corporation.* But as you'll see below, choosing S corporation status is a tax, not a legal, election—the same legal rules applicable to C corporations also apply to S corporations.

**TIP**

**LLCs have largely replaced S corporations.** The S corporation used to be the only structure that gave all owners of a business personal liability protection and pass-through taxation of business income. Since the arrival of the LLC, S corporations have largely fallen out of favor. That's because the LLC provides substantially the same benefits as an S corporation without several of the significant restrictions. (I discuss these below.)

## Number of Shareholders (Owners) and Directors

Generally, an S corporation may have no more than 100 shareholders, all of whom must be either (1) individuals who are U.S. citizens or residents, or (2) certain types of trusts or estates. The 100-shareholder limit may not be much of an inconvenience—most small businesses have fewer than five owners—but the other shareholder restrictions can be significant.

## Limited Liability for Shareholders

Like C corporations, all S corporation shareholders have limited personal liability protection from the debts and other liabilities of the corporation.

## Paying Taxes

Once a corporation makes an S corporation tax election, its profits and losses pass through the corporation and are reported on the individual tax returns of the S corporation's shareholders. This means that any profits an S corporation retains at the end of the year are not taxed at corporate tax rates—as is the case for a regular C corporation—but are passed through to the S corporation's owners. These profits are allocated and taxed to each shareholder each year at the shareholder's individual income tax rates (again, this is the same basic pass-through tax treatment afforded partnership and LLC owners).

## S Corporations Compared to LLCs

Before the LLC business form came along, forming an S corporation was the preferred way for business owners to obtain personal liability protection while retaining pass-through taxation of business income. However, now that the LLC is on the scene, S corporations no longer hold much allure for most business owners. Here's why:

- **S corporation formation.** To form an S corporation, you must first form a corporation then elect S corporation tax treatment by filing an S corporation tax election with the IRS. This involves more paperwork than simply forming an LLC.

- **S corporation limited liability.** S corporation shareholders, like LLC members, are protected from personal liability for the debts of the business. But to keep this limited liability protection, you have to follow the corporate rules when running your business. This means issuing stock, electing officers, holding regular board of directors' and shareholders' meetings, keeping corporate minutes of all meetings, and following the other mandatory rules in your state's corporation code. By contrast, if you form an LLC, you don't have to jump through most of these legal hoops— you just make sure your management team is in agreement on major decisions and go about your business. Although it makes sense to hold formal LLC meetings from time to time to record important management decisions, *you* get to decide when this is really necessary.

- **S corporation ownership restrictions.** Because only individuals who are U.S. citizens or residents can own its stock, an S corporation doesn't have the same organizational flexibility of the LLC. (Special types of trusts and other special entities can own shares too, but these exceptions don't help the average business person.) Even if an S corporation initially meets the U.S. citizen (or resident) requirement, its shareholders can never sell shares to a foreign citizen or to a company (like a corporation or an LLC), or they will lose their corporation tax status. This also means that some of the C corporation's main benefits—namely the ability to set up stock option and bonus plans and to bring in public capital with an IPO—are pretty much out of the question. In an LLC, any type of person or entity can become a member— a U.S. citizen, a citizen of a foreign country, another LLC, a corporation, or a limited partnership.

- **S corporation allocation of profits and losses.** Because an S corporation cannot set up more than one class of stock (an exception is provided to allow it to issue voting and nonvoting shares), the corporation's profits and losses must be distributed to the shareholders in proportion to their stockholdings. LLCs have more flexibility in this regard, because they can tailor the allocations of profits and losses to meet the needs of investors. For example, an LLC can bring in an investor for a share of LLC profits or losses that's disproportionately larger than his or her capital interest.

EXAMPLE: Ely and Natalie want to go into business designing solar-powered hot tubs. Ely is the "money" person and agrees to pitch in 80% of the funds necessary to get the business going. Natalie is the hot tub and solar specialist and will operate the business. One-half of Natalie's first-year salary, plus a cash payment of $20,000, will fund her initial 20% share in the enterprise, which she will buy at the end of the first year. Ely will receive two-thirds of the profits of the business for five years, at which point they will start to be divided equally. While doling out profits this way makes practical sense for Ely and Natalie, S corporation rules would not allow them to allocate profits in a way that doesn't match their ownership shares. Far better for Ely and Natalie to form an LLC, which does allow them this flexibility.

- **Limitations of S corporation tax treatment.** A full discussion of S corporation taxes is beyond the scope of this book. Nevertheless, I want to mention one aspect of S corporations that can make a huge difference to some business investors. Generally, an S corporation's business debts cannot be passed along to its shareholders unless they have personally loaned the money to the corporation. This means that the tax basis of an S corporation shareholder does not increase when the company takes on debt. In contrast, LLCs normally can give their owners the tax benefits of any business debt, meaning that their tax basis may increase when the company takes on debt. This increase in basis means that, in the short term, each of the LLC owners is less likely to be taxed on profits distributed to them by the LLC. If a company will incur substantial debt, as would often be the case if it borrows money to open its business or buy real estate, it might make more sense to form an LLC than an S corporation.

EXAMPLE: An LLC borrows $400,000. This debt is allocated equally to the four LLC owners. This means it increases the basis each owner holds in his or her capital (ownership) interest. This basis increase, in turn, means that each owner can receive up to $100,000 in distributions of profits from the LLC without being taxed (distributions are taxed only when they exceed an owner's basis). By contrast, S corporation shareholders typically do not receive an increased basis in their shares when the corporation borrows money, so a loan of this sort would not provide a tax benefit to them.

SEE AN EXPERT

**Benefits of entity-level debt.** This a highly technical area. If you want more information, talk to a tax adviser.

CAUTION

**S corporations have an advantage when it comes to self-employment taxes.** S corporation owners do enjoy one advantage over standard LLCs with respect to self-employment taxes (Social Security and Medicare taxes). S corporation shareholders normally do not have to pay self-employment taxes on S corporation profits that are allocated to them at the end of each year, over and above any actual salary they receive. The general rule for LLCs is that LLC members who are active in their business must pay self-employment taxes on profits allocated to them at the end of the year, which means that they may pay more self-employment taxes than if they had formed an S corporation.

EXAMPLE: Sam owns a one-person S corporation that nets $250,000 in profits (before payment of Sam's salary). Sam pays himself $100,000 in salary, and the remaining $150,000 is allocated to him at the end of the year as a profit on his investment. Because an S corporation is a pass-through tax entity, all of this money is credited to Sam for tax purposes. Sam pays income taxes and self-employment taxes only on the first $100,000; for the next $150,000, he pays only income taxes, not self-employment taxes. By contrast, if Sam had organized his business as a one-person LLC, he would normally have to pay self employment taxes on the entire amount. Of course, paying this extra amount may be in Sam's long-term self-interest because, if he pays more funds into his Social Security account now, he stands to receive a larger monthly Social Security benefit when he retires.

## Disadvantages of the S Corporation Compared to the C Corporation

The S corporation's ownership restrictions and its inability to issue special classes of stock also makes the S corporation a lot less flexible than a regular C corporation when it comes to attracting key employees and investment capital—two of the advantages a regular C corporation enjoys as compared to an LLC. Because an S corporation cannot have more than 100 shareholders, it can't make a public offering of its shares. And, because an S corporation must have one class of shares, it can't easily accommodate the needs of outside venture capital firms and other investors who require special dividend or conversion rights in return for a capital investment in a company.

TIP

**An LLC can elect S corporation taxation.** Some LLC owners decide to change their LLC into an S corporation to save money on self-employment taxes. See Chapter 4 for more on this.

# What Is an RLLP?

In all 50 states, professionals may set up a special type of partnership, called a limited liability partnership (LLP) or a registered limited liability partnership (RLLP), as an alternative to forming an LLC. In a few states (California, for example), this new type of ownership structure was invented because state law didn't allow many professionals to form LLCs. In others, this business structure was established to help professionals in a multi-member practice avoid personal liability for the malpractice of the other professionals in their firm. If you are not forming a professional practice along with professional co-owners, the RLLP is probably not of interest to you.

An RLLP is essentially a partnership in which all of the owners remain personally liable for their own acts (malpractice), but receive limited liability for the malpractice of other partners in the firm. Most state RLLP statutes also give the professionals personal liability protection from other tort liabilities of the RLLP (slip-and-fall lawsuits, for example) as well as from business debts.

## Number of Partners

At least two partners are needed to form an RLLP. Typically, under state statutes, the partners must be licensed in the same or related professions. Usually professionals that are eligible to form an RLLP include people who work in the legal, medical, and accounting fields, as well as a short list of other professions in which a special "professional-client" relationship is assumed to exist.

> **TIP**
> **Professionals eligible to form professional corporations can usually form RLLPs.** The list of professionals who may form an RLLP is normally the same as the one used to determine which professionals are eligible to form a professional corporation under state law. For example, physicians can incorporate only as a professional corporation in most states, and are typically

also eligible to form an RLLP. Call your state LLC filing office to find out which professionals are eligible to form RLLPs in your state.

## Limited Liability

RLLP owners enjoy a benefit not available to the owners of other professional practice partnerships: While the owners remain liable for the financial consequences of their own malpractice, they are not liable for the malpractice of the other professionals in their partnership. In addition, in more than half of the 50 states, a partner in an RLLP is not personally liable for any type of liability, whether arising from contracts, torts, or the professional malpractice of another professional in the firm. This sort of sweeping protection is known as "full shield" limited liability protection.

Again, before forming an RLLP or converting an existing professional partnership to one, it's important to find out how much personal limited liability protection your state RLLP statute provides. In addition to reading your state's law yourself, one good way to do this is to consult your professional trade or licensing organization; they almost certainly keep up with the law in this area. If you are thinking of forming a multi-member professional practice, a knowledgeable business lawyer in your state can help you sort out just how much protection your state RLLP statute provides.

## Paying Taxes

Like partnerships and LLCs, RLLPs are taxed as pass-through tax entities. This means that the owners are taxed on all profits on their individual income tax returns at their individual tax rates; the RLLP itself is not taxed on profits. In most professional firms that provide services rather than goods, all profits are usually available to be paid out to the professionals each year—there is normally little need to accumulate funds in professional service firms (as there often is in a nonservice business that needs to accumulate earnings for inventory, equipment, or future expansion).

## RLLPs Compared to LLCs

For practical purposes, RLLPs are very similar to LLCs. They both have pass-through taxation; they both provide limited personal liability. In some states, one difference is that RLLP statutes usually protect professionals from legal liability for the malpractice of their partners, while some LLC statutes do not. This is not normally a problem for the typical LLC owner—legal liability in most businesses comes about as a result of contract disputes, accidents on the premises (for example, slip-and-fall injuries), customer or product complaints, and the like—not as a result of an owner's direct, negligent injury of a client. But of course, in a professional practice, things are very different; professionals are routinely sued for alleged direct or indirect harm caused by the professional's own actions or omissions.

One other difference between the LLC and the RLLP has to do with their ability to distribute profits freely. Many professional firms want to be able to distribute all net profits of the business to its owners. After all, most professional firms offer services, not goods, and do not need to keep profits in the company to stock inventory or expand the enterprise. But, under most state LLC (and corporate) laws, LLCs cannot make distributions to owners if doing so would make the business insolvent—that is, unable to pay its debts as they become due—or would make the business's liabilities exceed its assets by a certain percent. An RLLP normally has no such limitations. However, many LLCs will not want to distribute every last penny of profits to owners each year, so these technical limitations will have little significance for them.

# The Series LLC

A new type of LLC is taking shape under state LLC laws: the series LLC. A growing number of states currently allow business owners to form a series LLC. To find out if your state is among them, go to your state's LLC filing office online (see Appendix A for contact information).

The defining characteristic—and main advantage—of the series LLC (SLLC) is that it allows business owners to form one LLC to run separate businesses or properties. Each individual series is administratively separate from the rest. This means separate businesses can be subsumed into one LLC entity, but the business and assets of each series can be managed and operated separately. For example, each series can have separate owners and managers, a separate operating agreement that specifies a separate division of profits and losses associated with the series, and other separate formation and operation characteristics.

Some states that allow series LLCs provide that each series is insulated from the liabilities of the other series within the LLC. In these states, assets (such as real estate) can be put into separate series within an LLC, and each property will be subject only to its own financing obligations (mortgages, equity lines of credit, and the like), not the financing obligations of property placed within other series. This consolidation of assets in one LLC coupled with a separation of liability between the assets in each series can be an advantage to organizers who want to set up one LLC to develop, encumber, and sell multiple parcels of real estate.

Before you jump on the series LLC bandwagon, however, there are several cautions to keep in mind. For one, a state that does not have a series LLC statute may not respect the special characteristics of a series LLC formed in another state. Even if a state allows for the formation of a series LLC, it may not offer all of the same legal protections granted under another state's series LLC statute.

And there are other uncertainties. For example, it is not clear that a federal bankruptcy court will respect the separation of each series within an LLC. If one series in an LLC files for bankruptcy, the court might reach out and grab the assets of the other series in the LLC to satisfy claims filed by creditors of the bankrupt series.

Some entrepreneurs may want to form a series LLC to avoid paying formation and annual fees for multiple LLC entities. For example, if one series LLC is formed for six separate properties, the organizers will pay one filing fee when the LLC is formed, not six. However, some states may not be willing to forgo those filing fees so easily. For example, the California Franchise Tax Board, which assesses an $800 franchise tax payment plus an annual added "total income" fee of up to $12,000 per year on each LLC formed or operating within the state, has said that it will treat each individual series of an out-of-state SLLC as a separate LLC. This means that a Delaware series LLC that operates in California will have to pay the annual California franchise and any added tax for *each* series within the LLC. Similarly, when you go to register your series LLC in a state that does not have a series LLC statute, the state may decide that you owe a registration fee for each series in your LLC, not just one for the whole LLC.

It will take time for the states to develop their series LLC statutes and to coordinate the laws, fees, and tax treatments.

## Do-Good LLCs and Corporations— The Latest in Limited Liability Entities

A growing number of states allow the formation of hybrid entities (LLCs and/or corporations) that can make a profit yet also do good. For example, Wyoming authorizes the formation of "low-profit LLCs" (also called L3Cs) that can be formed for an educational or charitable purpose but also can make a profit. As another example, California allows the formation of "flexible purpose corporations" and "benefit corporations," which can be formed to do good works as well as to make money. The advantage of these hybrid entities is that they can allow the principals to spend time and money trying to do good without having to worry about stakeholders' being upset (and suing them) for not spending all their time trying to turn a profit. These hybrids are sometimes loosely referred to as "B" corporations but, in fact, "B corporation" status is a separate, private (not state-law sanctioned) classification, which can be attained by any type of entity (not just a corporation). If you want to learn more about them, search for "B corporations" online or just go to www.bcorporation.net.

# Deciding Between an LLC and Another Business Type

Now that you know some basic information on each business structure, you can make some preliminary decisions about which types of legal entity might work for your business—and which might not.

## Businesses That May Benefit From the LLC Structure

LLCs generally work best for:

- **Businesses with a limited number of active owners.** In an LLC, all of the business owners are able to enjoy limited liability and have a full hand in LLC management. This said, it's also true that member-managed LLCs work best when there are relatively few owners. (See Chapter 1 for a lengthier discussion of how many members are practical in an LLC.) True, a larger LLC can limit the number of cooks in the kitchen by adopting a manager-management structure, where a select group of members manage the LLC on behalf of a larger, inactive membership. However, establishing a more complex manager-managed LLC does require additional thought and paperwork, and could bring up securities issues (see Chapter 5 for a discussion of the manager-management option). As an alternative, companies with more than 15 or 20 owners and investors may be better off forming a corporation.

- **Businesses that want to split profits and losses flexibly without an extra level of income taxation.** LLC members can split up profits and losses pretty much any way they want to (subject to special IRS rules), plus they have only one level of income taxation to deal with. If LLC owners start making more money each year than they need or want to take out of the company, and they want to shelter it in the business at lower corporate income tax rates, they can elect corporate income tax treatment for their LLC.

- **Start-up companies that may lose money.** New businesses often lose money in their first year or two. That explains why start-ups want the ability to pass early-year losses along to owners to deduct against their other income (usually salary earned working for another company or income earned from investments). Fortunately, LLC members can deduct their LLC losses against other income (assuming they meet all the IRS rules).

- **Companies that aren't 100% insured.** Especially if your enterprise is at risk of being sued by customers, employees, suppliers, members of the public, or competitors, and you can't afford to fully insure yourself against all of these risks, you'll want to protect your personal assets against the threat posed by lawsuits. Unless your business needs to raise money from a number of investors or plans to go public, the best way to do this is to form an LLC.

- **Existing sole proprietorships or general partnerships.** If you are self-employed—full or part time—or you own or operate an unincorporated business with others, you may worry that even though things are going well, a business reverse or just an unlucky accident could result in a business-breaking debt. Even though the chances of this occurring may be small, you still worry. One of the best ways to restore your peace of mind is to take a few minutes to fill out LLC articles and file them with your state. Once you do, your personal assets are legally off-limits when it comes to paying off business debts. And to get this benefit, you don't have to change your current income tax filing status. Further, the changeover is not normally a taxable event under IRS rules, just a change in your way of doing business. Simply put, converting your existing one- or multi-owner business to an LLC is a quick and legal way to give yourself an extra measure of needed assurance.

- **Anyone thinking of forming an S corporation.** To a large extent, the LLC was invented to streamline and fix things that were clunky or broken in the S corporation. The upshot is that LLC members more easily get the same limited liability protection as S corporation shareholders, and perhaps a more advantageous form of pass-through tax treatment.

## Businesses That May Not Benefit From the LLC Structure

LLCs generally work less well for:

- **Businesses without debt or liability risks.** If you are thinking of starting a very small business that is unlikely to experience a problem that will be solved by forming an LLC, then don't form one. For instance, a freelance proofreader who works at home and doesn't ever anticipate needing a loan to run his or her business probably doesn't need the limited liability that an LLC offers. Making a profit is hard enough—there is no sense in further complicating your life if you don't need to.

- **Professional firms.** If you are a professional in a multi-member firm, an RLLP may better protect you from personal liability for the malpractice of other professionals in your firm. Also, in some states, such as California, certain professionals are not allowed to form LLCs. In those states, their only choices are to form an RLLP or a professional corporation.

- **Capital-intensive and fast-track start-ups.** If your company expects to seek outside investment capital, offer equity-sharing plans to employees, or undertake a public offering of its stock, the corporate form is your best choice.

# Business Structures Comparison Table

The tables below highlight and compare the legal and tax traits of each type of business ownership structure. I've included a few extra technical issues to pique your interest. Should any of the additional points of comparison seem relevant to your particular business operation, talk them over with a legal or tax professional.

## Business Structures Comparison Table—Legal Characteristics

| | Sole Proprietorship | General Partnership | Limited Partnership | C Corporation | S Corporation | LLC |
|---|---|---|---|---|---|---|
| **Who owns business?** | sole proprietor | general partners | general and limited partners | shareholders | same as C corporation | members |
| **Personal liability for business debts** | sole proprietor personally liable | general partners personally liable | only general partner(s) personally liable | no personal liability of shareholders | same as C corporation | no personal liability of members |
| **Restrictions on kind of business** | may engage in any lawful business | may engage in any lawful business | same as general partnership | some states prohibit formation of banking, insurance, and other special businesses | same as C corporation, but excessive passive income (such as from rents, royalties, interest) can jeopardize tax status if converted from C corporation | same as C corporation |
| **Restrictions on number of owners** | only one sole proprietor | minimum two general partners | minimum one general partner and one limited partner | most states allow one-person corporations; some require two or more directors and/or officers | same as C corporation, but no more than 100 shareholders permitted | all states allow one-person LLCs |
| **Who makes management decisions?** | sole proprietor | general partners | general partner(s) only (not limited partners) | board of directors | same as C corporation | members; managers if manager-managed LLC |
| **Who may legally obligate business?** | sole proprietor | any general partner | any general partner (not limited partners) | directors and officers | same as C corporation | ordinarily any member; any manager if manager-managed LLC |

## Business Structures Comparison Table—Legal Characteristics, continued

| | Sole Propri-etorship | General Partner-ship | Limited Partner-ship | C Corporation | S Corporation | LLC |
|---|---|---|---|---|---|---|
| **Effect on business if an owner dies or departs** | dissolves automati-cally | dissolves automati-cally unless otherwise stated in partnership agreement | same as general partnership | no effect | same as C corporation | no effect unless only remaining owner departs (in most states) |
| **Limits on transfer of ownership interests** | free transfer-ability | consent of all partners usually required under partnership agreement | same as general partnership | transfer of stock may be limited under securities laws or restrictions in articles of incorporation or bylaws | same as C corporation, but transfers limited to persons and entities that qualify as S corporation shareholders | unanimous consent of nontrans-ferring members may be required under state law or operating agreement |
| **Amount of organi-zational paperwork and ongo-ing legal formalities** | minimal | minimal; partnership agreement recom-mended | start-up filing required; partnership agreement recom-mended | start-up filing required; bylaws recom-mended; annual meet-ings of share-holders usually required | same as C corporation | start-up filing required; operating agreement recom-mended; meet-ings not normally required |
| **Source of start-up funds** | sole proprietor | general partners | general and limited partners | initial shareholders (in some states, cannot invest with promise to perform services or contribute cash in the future) | same as C corporation, but cannot issue different classes of stock with different financial provisions | members (usually may invest with promise to perform services or contribute cash in the future) |

## Business Structures Comparison Table—Legal Characteristics, continued

| | Sole Proprietorship | General Partnership | Limited Partnership | C Corporation | S Corporation | LLC |
|---|---|---|---|---|---|---|
| **How business usually obtains capital, if needed** | sole proprietor's contributions; working capital loans backed by personal assets of sole proprietor | capital contributions from general partners; business loans from banks backed by partnership and personal assets | investment capital from limited partners; bank loans backed by general partners' personal assets | flexible; outside investors (may offer various classes of shares); bank loans backed by shareholders' personal assets (if corporation has insufficient credit history); may go public if need substantial infusion of cash | generally same as C corporation, but can't have foreign or partnership corporate shareholders; must limit number of shareholders to 100; can't offer different classes of stock to investors except for shares without voting rights | capital contributions from members; bank loans backed by members' personal assets (if LLC has insufficient credit history) |
| **Ease of conversion to another business form** | may change form at will; legal paperwork may be involved | may change to limited partnership, corporation, or LLC; legal paperwork involved | may change to corporation or LLC; legal paperwork involved | may change to S corporation by filing simple tax election; change to LLC can involve tax cost and legal complexity | generally same as C corporation; may terminate S tax status to become C corporation but cannot reelect S status for five years after | may change to general or limited partnership or corporation; legal paperwork involved |

## Business Structures Comparison Table—Legal Characteristics, continued

| | Sole Proprietorship | General Partnership | Limited Partnership | C Corporation | S Corporation | LLC |
|---|---|---|---|---|---|---|
| **Is establishment or sale of ownership interests subject to federal and state securities laws?** | generally not | generally not | issuance or sale of limited partnership interests must qualify for securities laws exemptions; otherwise must register with federal and state securities laws offices | issuance or transfer of stock subject to state and federal securities laws or must qualify for securities laws exemptions | same as C corporation | probably not, if all members are active in business |
| **Who generally finds this the best way to do business?** | owner who wants legal and managerial autonomy | joint owners who are not concerned with personal liability for business debts | joint owners who want partnership tax treatment and some non-managing investors; general partners must be willing to assume personal liability for business debts | owners who want limited liability and ability to split income between themselves and a separately taxed business | owners who want limited liability and individual tax rates to apply to business income; must be willing to meet initial and ongoing S corporation requirements | owners who want limited liability and pass-through taxation; particularly beneficial for smaller, privately held businesses |
| **How business profits are taxed** | individual tax rates of sole proprietor | individual tax rates of general partners | individual tax rates of general and limited partners | split up and taxed at corporate rates and individual tax rates of shareholders | individual tax rates of shareholders | individual tax rates of members |

## Business Structures Comparison Table—Legal Characteristics, continued

| | Sole Proprietorship | General Partnership | Limited Partnership | C Corporation | S Corporation | LLC |
|---|---|---|---|---|---|---|
| **Tax-deductible fringe benefits available to owners who work in business** | sole proprietor may set up IRA or Keogh retirement plan; can deduct medical insurance premiums | general partners and other employees may set up IRA or Keogh plans; can deduct medical insurance premiums | same as general partnership | full tax-deductible fringe benefits for employee-shareholders; may deduct medical and term-life insurance premiums and reimburse employees' medical expenses | same as general partnership, but employee-shareholders owning 2% or more of stock are restricted from corporate fringe benefits under partnership rules | can get benefits associated with sole proprietorship, partnership, or corporation, depending on tax treatment of LLC |
| **Automatic tax status** | yes | yes | yes, upon filing certificate of limited partnership with state corporate filing office | yes, upon filing articles of incorporation with state corporate filing office | no; must meet requirements and file tax election form with IRS (and sometimes state); revoked or terminated tax status cannot be reelected for five years | yes, with IRS, unless LLC wishes to elect corporate tax treatment (by filing IRS Form 8832); most states treat LLC as IRS does for state income tax purposes |

## Business Structures Comparison Table—Legal Characteristics, continued

| | Sole Proprietorship | General Partnership | Limited Partnership | C Corporation | S Corporation | LLC |
|---|---|---|---|---|---|---|
| **Are taxes due when business is formed?** | generally tax-free to set up | generally tax-free to set up; individual income taxes may be due if a general partner contributes services as capital contribution | usually same as general partnership | generally not taxable if requirements of Internal Revenue Code § 351 are met | same as C corporation | generally tax-free to set up; individual income taxes may be due if a member contributes services as capital contribution |
| **Deductibility of business losses** | owner may deduct losses from other income on individual tax returns (subject to active-passive investment loss rules that apply to all businesses) | partners may deduct losses from other income on individual tax returns if "at risk" for loss or debt, to extent of partner's tax basis in partnership interest | same as general partnership, but limited partners may only deduct "nonrecourse debts" (for which general partners are not specifically liable) | corporation may deduct business losses; shareholders may not | shareholders may deduct share of corporate losses on individual tax returns, subject to special limitations | follows sole proprietorship, partnership, or corporate loss rules depending on tax status of LLC |

## Business Structures Comparison Table—Legal Characteristics, continued

|  | Sole Proprietorship | General Partnership | Limited Partnership | C Corporation | S Corporation | LLC |
|---|---|---|---|---|---|---|
| **Tax rate when business is sold** | personal tax rate of owner | personal tax rate of individual general partners | personal tax rate of individual general and limited partners | two rates: shareholders and corporation may be taxed on liquidation if it includes sale or transfer of appreciated property | normally taxed at personal tax rates of individual shareholders, but corporate rate tax sometimes due if S corporation was formerly a C corporation | follows sole proprietorship, partnership, or corporate tax rules depending on tax status of LLC |

# Members' Capital and Profits Interests

I n this chapter, I look at the financial arrangements typically used to set up an LLC and divide LLC profits and losses among the LLC owners (members). I also discuss some of the basic tax ramifications associated with these arrangements.

Let's start with some background on how most start-up LLCs are funded—that is, how the organizers of a new LLC pay capital into their business. Of course, these start-up considerations don't loom as large for existing businesses, such as sole proprietorships and partnerships, that are converting their organizations to LLCs. In that case, the assets of the existing business simply carry over to the LLC, usually with no change in the owners' capital interests and profits and loss interests, or in the tax positions of the business owners (see "Converting an Existing Business to an LLC," below).

## LLC Capital Interests

The initial members of a new LLC ordinarily make financial contributions (called "capital contributions" in business lingo) to the business to get it started. These contributions can consist of:

- cash
- property
- services, or
- a promise to contribute cash, property, or services in the future.

In return, each LLC member normally gets a percentage of owner-ship in the assets of the LLC (this is called a member's "capital interest"). This interest reflects the portion of the LLC assets that the member is entitled to if the member sells his or her membership interest or the LLC itself is sold. For example, if a member has a 50% capital interest in an LLC with assets, including goodwill, valued at $500,000, that member can expect to be paid approximately $250,000 if the other members buy out his or her interest. Of course, a good LLC operating agreement (or buy-sell agreement) will clearly explain how members' interests will be valued so that members can anticipate how much they'll get in exchange for their interest and when they'll get it (in a lump sum, installment payments, or a combination of the two).

EXAMPLE 1: Tim, Dan, and Ellory are about to form Home Page Designs, a website development company. The capital necessary to start the LLC is minimal, and all three expect to contribute an equal amount of work in operating the enterprise. Tim plans to contribute his sophisticated, power-user computer equipment, worth $12,000, and Dan plans to contribute $12,000 in cash, enough to buy two scaled-down workstations for himself and Ellory. Ellory, who doesn't have any ready cash or property, agrees to contribute $12,000 by simply leaving the first $12,000 of his share of allocated profits in the business. The three become equal one-third owners of the LLC, each with a one-third capital interest in the company.

EXAMPLE 2: After reading "Tax Considerations of Start-Up Capital," below, Ellory realizes that he may have to pay income tax on the value of his capital interest if he contributes services to the LLC. Instead, he asks the other owners if they will extend a personal loan to him of $12,000 cash, which he will use to buy a one-third interest in the LLC. He agrees to pay back the personal loan, with interest, from his share of LLC profits earned during the first year of LLC operations.

# Tax Considerations of Start-Up Capital

As you can see from the above examples, members may make capital contributions to their LLC in the form of cash, property, and/or services, or the promise to provide any of these in the future. However, any member who contributes property or services rather than cash should be aware of several important tax considerations, discussed below.

## Paying With Cash

If your LLC members simply contribute cash to start up your LLC, the tax considerations are straightforward. The members are not taxed on the transaction. Instead, their membership interest receives an "income tax basis" equal to the amount of cash each member invests. This tax basis will go up and down during the life of the LLC as profits and losses are allocated and paid to members and as the LLC's liabilities fluctuate. When a member finally sells his or her membership interest or the LLC itself is sold, the tax basis at that time will be used to compute the amount of gain that the member owes taxes on.

> EXAMPLE: Jethro pays $1,000 to start his gold-panning LLC in the Sierra mountain foothills. He buys an inexpensive silt strainer, then sets up camp by a small stream, spending his days slowly sifting for gold and daydreaming of future wealth and luxury. A year later, when he sells his LLC to his cousin Ned for $2,000, his income tax basis still sits at $1,000. This means Jethro's taxable gain on the sale is $1,000, which is the amount on which he must pay capital gains taxes.

## Paying With Property

Another popular way to fund an LLC is through the contribution of property. For example, a member may transfer title to a piece of real estate to the LLC in return for a membership interest. Vehicles, business equipment, and machinery, as well as patents and trademarks, are also commonly exchanged for membership interests. As long as other LLC members (if there are any) accept the property at an agreed-upon value, there is no legal impediment to doing this. But in some circumstances, contributions of property (especially property that has appreciated in value) can lead to special tax consequences.

### Transferring Appreciated Property

Tax issues arise when a member contributes property that has increased in value (appreciated) since the member bought, inherited, or received it as a gift. This is most likely when a member contributes real estate. First, the good news: Contributions of appreciated property to an LLC are generally tax free when they are made (there are some technical exceptions, of course—see below). The not-so-good news is that a member who transfers appreciated property to the LLC must eventually pay taxes on the past appreciation (the increase in value that occurred before the member transferred the property to the LLC). Typically, the member who originally transferred the property to the LLC pays taxes on the past appreciation when his or her interest in the LLC, or the entire LLC itself, is sold.

> **EXAMPLE:** Jim owns a building he bought outright for $20,000. It is worth $120,000 when he transfers it to his newly formed LLC (in other words, it has appreciated $100,000 since the date of purchase). In exchange for transferring this real estate to the LLC, Jim receives a capital stake in his LLC worth $120,000, based on the property's current fair market value. Jim's tax basis in his membership interest is $20,000—his "cost basis" in the transferred property. (This simplified example assumes there have been no adjustments to his basis in the property for capital improvements or depreciation.) Jim pays no taxes when he transfers the property to the LLC.
>
> Jim sells his membership interest for $120,000. (For simplicity's sake, let's assume his interest is worth the same amount when he sells it as when he transferred it to the LLC.) His gain—the amount he'll have to pay capital gains taxes on—is the amount he receives for his LLC interest ($120,000) minus his basis in the membership interest ($20,000). In other words, Jim has to report a gain of $100,000 and pay taxes on that amount at the time of the sale. As you can see, Jim doesn't avoid paying taxes on appreciation by transferring his building to the LLC; he simply defers paying them until later.

There are, however, a couple of big exceptions to the general rule that there are no immediate tax consequences when appreciated property is transferred to an LLC. For one, if the LLC distributes profits to a member within two years after he or she contributes property to the LLC, the member may owe taxes on the appreciation when the distribution is made.

And, if the LLC sells the contributed property, or distributes it to another member, taxes may also be due. Ask your tax adviser for the details.

## Property Subject to Debt

SKIP AHEAD

**This section does not apply to one-person LLCs.** If you are the only member of your LLC, you can skip this next section. It applies only if you transfer some debt to your LLC, and the other LLC members are allocated a portion of it. In a single-member LLC, if you contribute property that's subject to debt, you'll be allocated all of the debt, so there'll be no change in your tax position.

If a member of a multi-member LLC contributes property subject to debt— for example, a building encumbered with a mortgage—there are immediate tax consequences for that member. To understand why, remember that LLC members share profits and losses (debts) with each other. So when a member transfers mortgaged property to the LLC, the debt is allocated among all LLC members, including the member who transfers the property. Typically, each member takes on a share of the debt that's in proportion to his or her profits and loss interest, or distributive share, discussed in "Profit and Loss Interests," below. This allocation of debt increases each member's tax basis in his or her interest, which, in turn, reduces the taxable gain that will occur later, when a member sells the interest.

Because the debt is now shared, the transferring owner owes less than before. The IRS treats this decrease in debt obligation as a payout of cash to that member. For example, if you transfer property worth $100,000 to your LLC to become one of five equal members in the LLC, and the LLC assumes the $50,000 mortgage attached to the property, the IRS treats the transaction as though you were paid income of $40,000 (the amount of the mortgage assumed by the four other LLC members, or 4/5 of $50,000). You are obligated to pay tax on this amount if it exceeds your current income tax basis in your membership interest. Detailed rules in this area are too complicated to explain more fully here. Just be sure to talk to your accountant if you're considering transferring debt-burdened property to an LLC.

RESOURCE

**Helpful LLC tax resources.** Most books and articles that cover the tax consequences of LLC and partnership taxation assume a substantial amount of prior knowledge, and do a poor job of explaining the basic terms and concepts necessary to fully appreciate the material they cover. One exception is Prentice Hall's *Federal Taxation: Comprehensive* book, updated annually. It is used primarily as a text for students entering the tax field, and may be available at a local business or law library. It doesn't contain many fully developed examples of how the tax rules apply to smaller businesses, but you can use the material to get a basic understanding of the fundamental tax concepts that apply to an LLC, partnership, or corporation.

## Paying With Services

Sometimes an LLC member receives a capital interest in an LLC in return for personal services already performed or for a promise to perform services in the future (often in addition to a cash payment). For example, a member might pay $10,000 and promise to do 500 hours of work (without pay) to set up the LLC's website. The IRS views this type of transaction as "payment for services." This means the member must pay income taxes on the value of the membership interest received in exchange for the work, just as he or she would if the LLC had issued a paycheck for those hours of work. Whenever LLC members sign an operating agreement that issues a capital interest to a member in exchange for services, that member must pay income tax for the value of those services as recorded on the LLC's books.

> **EXAMPLE:** Five Austin computer programmers start Computer Tex, LLC. Four put up $20,000 each as their 20% capital contributions. In return, they each get a 20% capital interest in the LLC (their membership interest). Cash-strapped Sharon, the fifth member, receives her 20% membership interest in exchange for a promise to do certain programming work for the company without pay. The IRS considers this payment to be personal service

income to Sharon. She'll owe individual income taxes on the $20,000, and she'll have to estimate and pay it during the year even though she never pockets a nickel.

**SEE AN EXPERT**

**Contact a tax expert if a member will pay for a membership interest with services or property instead of cash.** Paying for an LLC membership interest with services or property can create complications, and the above examples are simply meant to introduce you to these areas. Please consult your tax adviser if you or another member is thinking of paying for an interest with services or property.

**CAUTION**

**Proposed IRS rules on paying for an LLC interest with services.** Under proposed Treasury Regulation 105346-03, LLCs and their owners must follow special rules, adopt special agreements, and make sure that special tax elections are filed by members who receive partnership (and LLC) interests in return for the performance of services. These requirements must be met within 30 days of the issuance of the interests to obtain favorable tax treatment. Make sure to ask your tax adviser how to comply with these and the other special rules and requirements before you decide to issue profits or other LLC interests in return for the performance of services.

## Paying With Borrowed Money

Fortunately, there are several ways that a member who doesn't have cash or property to contribute can get around the tax consequences of contributing services.

One approach is for the member to borrow the needed cash, then buy a capital interest outright. The loan can be from an outside source, such as a bank, another LLC member, or even the LLC itself (if your state's LLC law allows LLCs to issue a membership in exchange for a promissory note—see Appendix A for information on looking up your state's law). The member who receives the loan signs a promissory note specifying repayment terms, including a competitive, commercially reasonable interest rate. The member can pay back the loan with payments of profits from the LLC or some other source of funds. Of course, depending on the lender's requirements, the member may also be required to pledge property as security for repayment.

> **EXAMPLE:** Bella and Xavier kick around the idea of forming Happy Hoofs Equestrian Academy LLC—a proposed horse-riding and boarding facility in the rolling foothills of Mesa de Oro, California. Bella can contribute the cash and property to finance a down payment on a pleasantly weather-worn barn with surrounding acreage, and otherwise get the business off and happily running. But Xavier, who is champing at the bit with energy that he'll use to convert the farm to a riding academy, is low on funds. Realizing that their venture is far more likely to succeed if Xavier is a co-owner—not just a hired hand—Bella agrees to lend Xavier the money to become a member of the LLC. This means Xavier will receive a capital interest in the LLC without having to immediately pay taxes on the value of the services he promises to perform. This way Xavier can share in the LLC's profits while repaying Bella over several years.

TIP

**It can be a bad idea to wait to buy a membership interest.** An obvious way to avoid paying income taxes on a capital interest received in exchange for services is for a member-wannabe to simply wait until he or she has earned sufficient cash to buy a membership interest. But if the LLC increases in value right off the bat, the member-wannabe may not be able to afford the increased cost of an interest in the business.

**Example:** Let's return to the Happy Hoofs Equestrian Academy LLC. Now assume Bella and her husband, Clyde, form the LLC as the two initial members. Xavier, who can't afford to become a member right away, works for the ranch as an employee and saves his money. Xavier plans to buy out Clyde's capital interest in the LLC when he has sufficient cash. Unfortunately for Xavier, the ranch becomes profitable quickly, and Xavier can't afford to pay Clyde the fair value of his capital interest, which has shot up in value since Bella and Clyde opened the Academy. Not only is Xavier unable to buy into a chunk of the LLC assets, but he also hasn't been able to share in its hefty profits while he's been working there.

## Receiving a Profits-Only Interest

An LLC member can also avoid having to pay taxes on the value of services if the LLC gives him or her a "profits-only" interest in the LLC (rather than an ownership interest in LLC assets) in return for a promise to render future services. Income taxes won't be due immediately, because a capital (ownership) interest won't be issued.

Technical note: Taxes may be due even when a profits-only interest is issued if the LLC has a predictable pattern of earning profits—most LLCs don't have surefire profits, so this isn't normally a problem. Of course, like any member, the member with the profits-only interest must pay taxes on LLC profits as they are allocated to him or her. And taxes may also be due if the member sells or transfers a profits interest within two years after it is issued.

> EXAMPLE: Hubert Allis Overalls, Ltd. Co., which supplies denim fabric to clothing manufacturers, brings in Hank Allis (son of founding member Hubert) to help run the LLC. Business is busting at the rivets, with the LLC supplying fabric to several brand-name jeans manufacturers. In return for signing a ten-year employment contract, Hank is given a 25% stake in LLC profits for that period, plus a guaranteed annual salary. Because Hank does not receive a capital interest in the LLC, he will not be taxed up front on his promise to perform services for the LLC.

Although a profits-only interest is a true economic interest in an LLC, it is not the same as a capital (ownership) interest, because it doesn't give the holder a right to a portion of LLC assets when the LLC is sold. Of course, if the business does well, the holder of a profits-only interest will benefit by sharing in the profits *until* the company is sold. Often, the holder of a profits-only interest buys a capital interest in the LLC as soon as he or she is financially able to do so—using profits earned in the meantime. Alternatively, the holder of a profits-only interest can sell that interest as long as the sale is not prohibited by the LLC's operating agreement, although the holder may not be able to find a buyer unless the LLC has a proven profit-making track record.

## Converting an Existing Business to an LLC

Many sole proprietors and partners decide to convert their existing business into an LLC. As discussed throughout this book, it's a quick and legal way for business owners to limit their personal liability for business debts and claims. These businesses already exist under a different legal structure, so it's no surprise that their owners fund their LLCs differently from the new LLCs discussed above. In most cases, the assets and liabilities of the existing business are simply transferred to the LLC, and the old owners take over as owners of the new business, with the same percentages of ownership they had in the old business.

> **EXAMPLE:** Imogene and Bethany convert their 50–50 partnership, Rugby Sales Group, into an LLC. They prepare an LLC operating agreement that gives each new LLC owner a 50% capital interest, plus a 50% distributive share of LLC profits and losses.

One nice part of converting an unincorporated business to an LLC is that it is not usually treated as a taxable sale, so the old business owners don't pay taxes as a result of the conversion. The IRS recognizes that converting a sole proprietorship or a partnership into an LLC is simply a change in the legal structure of an existing business, not a sale of assets from one business to another.

After converting an unincorporated business to an LLC, the business and its owners continue to file the same tax returns they filed prior to the conversion (for a sole proprietorship that converts to an LLC, a 1040 Schedule C; for a partnership that converts to an LLC, the 1065 partnership tax return).

When converting an existing business to an LLC, the owners should make sure to change the business's name on business licenses, permits, insurance policies, and titles to personal property and real estate. They also need to change their federal employer ID number (if they have one), their state employer registration number, and all other formal business numbers, licenses, and permits to the name of the new LLC. An LLC operating agreement should also be prepared, even if the owners don't change their percentages of capital interests, profits and losses, and management power. (For more on operating agreements, see Chapter 6.)

Converting a corporation to an LLC is far more difficult. And it can be costly, because there's often a substantial tax bite. In fact, after considering the difficulties and legal expenses involved, most corporation owners who want to get rid of their corporate tax status and be treated as pass-through tax entities create an S corporation instead (see Chapter 2 for more on S corporations). Indeed, allowing owners of existing C corporations to obtain pass-through tax status is one of the few remaining practical uses of the S corporation.

## Profit and Loss Interests

When LLC members receive a capital interest in an LLC in exchange for cash, property, or services, they also get a share of its profits and losses, called their "distributive share." You'll see the term "distributive share" a lot in IRS publications and tax forms: It refers to how much of the LLC's profits and losses will be allocated to each LLC owner at the end of the year. It is a bit of a misnomer, because under the pass-through tax rules an LLC's owners are taxed on all of the profits allocated to them at the end of each LLC tax year, even if these profits are not actually distributed. (I'll discuss the taxation of profit allocations and distributions in Chapter 4.) An owner's distributive share is sometimes also referred to as his or her "profits interest" in the LLC.

Each member's distributive share of profits and losses should be specified in the LLC operating agreement. Most often, an operating agreement will provide that each member's distributive share is the same as his or her capital interest in the LLC.

> EXAMPLE 1: Tony and Lisa set up Antler Artifacts, LLC, a retail outpost in Jackson Hole, Wyoming, that sells antler-shaped back scratchers, wapiti-musk potpourri, and other animal kingdom miscellany conscientiously made only with synthetic materials and resins. The two members contribute equal amounts of cash as start-up capital. The LLC operating agreement specifies that Tony's and Lisa's capital interests correspond to the amount of capital each contributed, and that their distributive shares of profits and losses are proportionate to their capital interests. Tony and Lisa contributed equal amounts of cash, so they each have a 50% capital interest and a 50% distributive share of LLC profits and losses.

If you do business as an LLC, your operating agreement can provide that profits and/or losses be distributed in a manner that is not proportionate to capital interests. For example, an LLC member with a 30% capital interest could receive 40% of the yearly profits. The ability to mete out allocations of profits and losses in different ways is one of the special advantages of setting up an LLC (or a partnership). By contrast, the founders of a corporation are unable to do this sort of disproportionate profit-splitting without a lot of tinkering with the standard corporate model. Allocating profits and losses in a way that is disproportionate to members' relative capital interests is called making "special allocations" under the tax law. Such divisions are subject to IRS tax rules, discussed in "Special Allocations of Profits and Losses," below.

EXAMPLE 2: Assume Tony and Lisa set up the same LLC, but this time Tony puts up all the cash, while Lisa signs a promissory note to contribute her share in installments over the first two years of the life of the LLC. Their operating agreement still says that Tony and Lisa each have a 50% capital interest, but it also says that Tony will be allocated 75% of the LLC's profits (and losses) for the first two years, while Lisa gets 25%. After the first two years, the agreement says that both members will split LLC allocations of profits and losses 50–50 (that is, according to the value of their capital interests). This setup constitutes a "special allocation of profits and losses" for the first two years, so their tax accountant included language in their operating agreement to make sure the IRS would respect the special allocation.

## Special Allocations of Profits and Losses

I promised you more information on special allocations of LLC profits and losses—and, because this is a technical area of the LLC rules, I saved it for last. Making special allocations of profits and losses will require you to get more detailed information than you'll find here, including professional tax advice.

As discussed throughout this book, LLC members can decide not to follow the usual practice of splitting up profits and losses proportionately to each member's capital interest when they form an LLC. Instead, they can agree to split profits and losses *disproportionately* to members' capital contributions by making what is called a "special allocation." For example, a special allocation would be necessary if an LLC allocates a 20% share of profits and losses to a member who contributes only 10% of the initial LLC cash or assets.

## "Substantial Economic Effect"

Unfortunately, the IRS regulations covering special allocations (Sections 1.704.1 through 1.704.3 of the Income Tax Regulations) go on for pages. Basically, these regulations state that special allocations of profits and losses are valid for tax purposes only if they have "substantial economic effect." This jargon means that special allocations must have a real economic impact on the person receiving the allocations; they can't just be an effort to avoid income tax. For example, if an LLC makes a special allocation that gives most of the losses to the owner who needs them most to lower his overall tax liability, the allocation must also affect the owner economically in a real way—namely, by lowering his capital account balance when the losses are allocated and requiring him to eventually pay back any losses that reduce his capital account below zero.

## Safe Harbor Rules for Special Allocations

If your LLC can follow the "safe harbor" rules that I discuss below— and, with the help of a tax specialist, adopt these rules in your operating agreement—you can ensure that any special allocations you make will have "substantial economic effect" for IRS purposes. The term "safe harbor" simply means that a business that follows these rules will be presumed to comply with tax or legal requirements.

The IRS lets you make special allocations (after you adopt the special safe harbor language in your operating agreement) primarily because there are some real financial and tax consequences to the owners who adopt this language. The language contains three basic requirements:

- **Maintenance of capital accounts.** The LLC's capital accounts must be carried and handled on the financial books according to special rules.
- **Liquidation of the LLC according to capital account balances.** Generally, your operating agreement must state that when your LLC is liquidated, assets will be distributed to the members in

accordance with their capital account balances. For example, if, at the termination of an LLC, Joe's capital account balance is $25,000 and Sam's $50,000, Joe should receive one-third of the assets and Sam should receive two-thirds.

- **Payback of negative capital account balances.** When an owner sells his or her interest, or the LLC is sold or liquidated, members with a negative capital account balance must restore their account to a zero balance. Capital accounts might go negative in any number of ways. For example, a member can be allocated losses in excess of his or her capital account balance, or distributions to a member can exceed the member's initial capital contribution plus profits that have been allocated but not paid out. A member can restore a negative capital account balance to zero by contributing cash or property to the LLC before the membership interest or the LLC itself is sold or liquidated. If you adopt this type of provision in your operating agreement, however, you have waived your limited liability protection, because you are personally agreeing to repay any deficit. You should think twice—and talk to your tax adviser—before making this decision.

There are a few ways to get around the last requirement to restore negative capital accounts, but they are beyond the scope of this overview book. Again, if you're interested in making special allocations, talk to your tax adviser.

SEE AN EXPERT

**Get help with special allocations.** Special allocations are tricky. Unless you want to get a degree in tax accounting, it's not something that most nonspecialists will want to tackle. The best way to adopt and implement these special allocation regulations is with the help of a very knowledgeable accountant—one who provides advice on pass-through tax law as a regular part of his or her practice and who can sort through the special allocation language to pick out the parts that you should include in your LLC operating agreement. Remember, if you agree to pay back a negative capital account balance, you could be personally liable to repay your LLC if it suffers a loss.

# Taxation of LLC Profits

This chapter explains the tax treatment that applies to LLCs under the current federal tax scheme. Fortunately, the basics of LLC taxation are straightforward and easy to grasp. There are, however, several areas of LLC taxation, such as electing corporate tax treatment, that can get complex in a hurry. I'll alert you to these more complicated areas, and I suggest that you check any preliminary conclusions you arrive at with a small business tax adviser before reaching any firm decisions about tax strategies for your LLC.

Believe it or not, one of the most exciting things about the LLC structure is its tax treatment. LLC legislators, lawyers, and accountants were not content to simply shake up small business law by successfully getting all states to legalize the LLC. They forged ahead and got the IRS to change the entire federal business classification system to enable an LLC (or a partnership) to elect to be taxed either as a pass-through entity (with income tax paid by LLC owners) or as a corporation. After covering the standard tax rules that apply to all new LLCs, I also discuss whether and when it might make sense for your LLC to choose corporate tax status.

## Pass-Through Tax Treatment

Unless you choose otherwise, pass-through income tax status is automatic for all new LLCs. This means that all of the LLC's profits and losses pass through the business and are reported and taxed on the owners' individual tax returns. But before I go further into income tax issues, let's discuss how LLC members pay themselves for actively working in or managing their business.

### Distributing Profits

In an unincorporated business like a partnership or a co-owned LLC, the owners share in the net profits of the business. They usually don't pay themselves a salary. Instead, each year (or often, each quarter), they see how much net profit remains after deducting all regular business expenses. Then they decide how much of this profit to distribute to themselves and how much to retain in the business. The next step is to calculate how much income must be allocated to each owner for income tax purposes according to each owner's "distributive share," or "profits interest," as set out in the LLC operating agreement. (See Chapter 3 for more on how this works.)

Even if some owners operate the business full time and others (passive investors) don't work in the business at all, the working/managing owners might not receive a salary. Instead, the working owners split the net profits with the passive owners according to their LLC operating agreement.

Of course, an LLC owner who works in the business may receive a salary or another type of guaranteed payment (one that doesn't depend on the LLC's profitability). This is particularly likely in a small business that produces profits year after year, or in a business where one managing owner does all the work for a group of passive investors. In this scenario, the working/managing owners may receive a guaranteed salary that is paid regardless of yearly fluctuations in the profit level of the business. Because the salary is guaranteed regardless of profits, it is a business expense and can be deducted by the business in computing its net profit. This, in turn, reduces the amount of profits the other owners are allocated and taxed on (of course, the other owners also receive less profits under this scenario). The working/managing owners who are paid salaries pay individual income taxes on the salary payouts plus, of course, their allocated share of any profits they divide with the other business owners. Before setting up a guaranteed payment for you or one of your co-owners, talk to your tax adviser.

## Pass-Through Taxation in a Nutshell

Now let's look at how LLC business profits are taxed. For a co-owned LLC, pass-through tax treatment means the LLC will be taxed as if it were a partnership. For a one-person LLC, it means the sole owner will be taxed as if he or she were a sole proprietor. In both instances, this means LLC profits will "pass through" the LLC and be allocated and taxed to the LLC owner or owners at the end of each LLC tax year. The

LLC owners, not the LLC itself, will be responsible for paying income taxes on business profits on their individual returns.

In a co-owned LLC, the amount of income allocated to each LLC member at the end of the year should be specified in the LLC's operating agreement (in a one-member LLC, of course, all income will pass through to the sole owner). Typically, each member in a co-owned LLC is allocated a percentage of LLC profits and losses that corresponds to the member's capital interest in the LLC, which, in turn, is usually based on the member's capital account balance in the LLC.

> **EXAMPLE:** Kirk contributes $10,000, and Scotty $20,000, to set up their LLC enterprise. The capital interests of these two members are stated in the form of membership units in the LLC operating agreement. Because both men will work full time in the business, but one has contributed twice as much as the other, the agreement states that Kirk owns 10,000 membership units and Scotty 20,000. The operating agreement further states that each member is allocated a percentage of LLC profits and losses (and management votes) that corresponds to his capital units. Therefore, Kirk gets one-third of the profits and losses and management voting power while Scotty receives two-thirds. Each pays individual income taxes on the amount of LLC profits allocated to him each year.

## Members Pay Income Taxes Even If They Aren't Paid Any Profits

While LLC members must pay individual taxes on all LLC net profits "allocated" to them each year under their operating agreement, their LLC is not required under the tax laws to distribute all—or, for that matter, any—of the LLC's profits at the end of the year. In other words, an owner's allocated profits are "earmarked" as belonging to that owner, but may or may not actually be distributed to that owner each year. Even if a member's allocated profits are retained by the LLC, the member must pay income taxes on those profits as if he or she received them. The IRS wants its income tax money each year; it doesn't want to wait until the LLC decides to put the money in the owners' pockets. If the owners were allowed to avoid taxes on profits by waiting until they felt like paying them out, you can be sure that in very good income years, when profits would cause LLC owners to be taxed in higher marginal tax brackets, owners would retain the profits in the business. Then in leaner years, when LLC owners would otherwise receive little or no income, they would pay them out so as to be taxed in lower individual tax brackets.

To deal with the potential problem of owing taxes on profits you don't receive, some LLC operating agreements contain a provision that says the owners must receive (actually have distributed to them) at least a minimum percentage (typically 25% to 35% or more) of their share of allocated profits each year. This gives each owner at least enough cash to pay individual income taxes and self-employment taxes on his or her share of allocated profits.

When it comes to actually paying out profits to the members, LLCs do have to pay attention to a few legal rules. In many states, there are financial tests that an LLC must meet before profits can be paid out. In general, a distribution of profits is valid if, after the distribution:

- the LLC remains solvent—that is, the LLC will be able to pay its bills as they become due in the normal course of business, and
- LLC assets remain equal to or exceed LLC liabilities (in some states, a statute sets out a higher asset-to-liability ratio that the LLC must be able to satisfy after distributing profits).

CAUTION
**Courts may ignore limited liability if these standards are ignored and the company is later sued.** Members or managers who approve a distribution in violation of statutory standards can be held liable for the amount of the invalid distribution. The moral here is, don't let your LLC pay out more profits to its owners than the business can afford.

## Pass-Through Taxation Compared to Corporate Taxation

To understand the practical implications of choosing pass-through treatment, you should also understand the basics of corporate tax treatment. The IRS taxes corporations, as well as unincorporated businesses that elect corporate tax treatment, in a fundamentally different way. Instead of passing all profits and tax liabilities through to its owners, the corporate business is taxed on the earnings and profits it retains in the business, while the owners are personally taxed only on profits they actually receive.

Payouts of profits in a corporation can be made in the form of salaries and bonuses to owners who work as employees of the business, or as dividends to owners who invest in the business. Payouts of profits as salaries and bonuses are tax-deductible business expenses, so the corporation doesn't pay taxes on them. They get taxed once—to the owner-employees at their individual income tax rates. By contrast, payouts of profits in the form of dividends are taxed twice—once to the corporation at the corporate tax rate (because they're not deductible expenses) and again to the owner to whom the dividends are paid, at special dividends tax rates. This rule explains why most small corporations rarely pay dividends.

This two-tiered level of taxation—in which the business pays taxes on retained profits while the owners pay taxes only on the profits they receive—results in a corporate tax benefit called "income splitting." Any profits left in the business (up to $75,000) will be taxed at the lowest corporate income tax rates of only 15% and 25%. These rates, of course, are often substantially lower than the individual tax rates that unincorporated business owners pay on the profits that are passed through to them. I'll have more to say about corporate income tax rates and income splitting in "Electing Corporate Tax Treatment," below.

Perhaps LLC pass-through tax treatment may appear inflexible as compared to corporate tax treatment. In some ways (for example, being taxed on all allocated profits), it is. But for most small businesses, this is not a bad thing. Here's why:

- Many LLC owners, especially if they're just starting out, pay out (distribute) all or most of the net business profits that are allocated to them each year. As a result, they end up paying taxes on money actually paid to them, just like the owners of a corporation. Because most LLC owners leave little or no earnings in the business at the end of the year, they're not paying taxes on money that they don't take home.

- Sole proprietors, partnerships, and S corporations, tax cousins to the LLC, are subject to the same set of pass-through tax rules. For owners who have experience operating one of these businesses, pass-through tax status is familiar and easy to work with.

- If an LLC becomes so profitable that there are profits left over after the owners take out enough for their own personal needs, or if an LLC needs to regularly keep substantial profits in the business to pay upcoming expenses, the LLC can elect to be taxed like a corporation. After this election is made, the owners are taxed only on profits actually paid to them, and the business pays corporate income taxes on any net profits left in the business. And, as mentioned above, because the initial corporate tax rates of 15% and 25% are lower than most individual tax rates, this ability to split income can result in tax savings. A corporate tax election has no effect on the LLC's legal status—the LLC remains an LLC for all purposes except taxes and can continue to operate under the procedural rules set up in its operating agreement. (I discuss this corporate tax treatment election in detail in "Electing Corporate Tax Treatment," below.)

## How LLCs Report and Pay Federal Income Taxes

If your LLC has only one member (and you haven't elected corporate tax treatment), the tax reporting process is simple. The LLC itself does not have to prepare and file any tax returns. The owner simply files his or her regular 1040 form and attaches Schedule C, *Profit or Loss From*

*Business (Sole Proprietorship)*, to report his or her share of allocated LLC profits or losses, and Schedule SE, *Self-Employment Tax*, to figure the self-employment (Social Security and Medicare) tax owed.

For LLCs with two or more owners, the LLC itself must prepare and file IRS Form 1065, the same tax form used by a partnership, unless it elects corporate tax treatment as explained below. LLCs themselves don't pay income taxes on profits (their owners do), so this annual partnership income return is informational only. Unfortunately, Form 1065 is a bit complicated for the uninitiated. To gather the necessary information, your business should use a standard double-entry bookkeeping system, with a journal of accounts that are periodically posted to a general ledger. These general ledger accounts, in turn, are used to generate an income statement and balance sheet, both of which are necessary to complete Form 1065. The form must also show a reconciliation of each owner's capital (ownership) account that shows his or her capital contributions and distributions as well as the allocations and distributions of profits to each owner.

Form 1065 also includes Schedule K, which reports the income, losses, credits, and deductions allocated to all owners. And finally, the LLC must give a Schedule K-1 form to each owner, on which it reports the profits, losses, credits, and deductions allocated to that owner— called the owner's "distributive share." Each owner uses the Schedule K-1, *Partner's Share of Income, Deductions, Credits, etc.,* to prepare an individual income tax return for the year and then attaches a copy of it to the 1040 form.

SEE AN EXPERT

**Use an accountant and/or a bookkeeper.** By now, if you are inexperienced in bookkeeping and accounting concepts, you may be a little daunted by the idea of setting up a double-entry tax reporting system. No question, it's a surprise to some when they first learn how complex the pass-through tax rules and procedures can be. So unless you have a good handle on basic accounting, consider hiring an accountant to help you set up a good system and a part-time bookkeeper to help maintain it.

> **RESOURCE**
>
> **A resource for operating your LLC.** For more information on how taxes and tax basis play out in ongoing LLC business transactions (for example, when an owner's interest is transferred or the business itself is sold), see my book, *Your Limited Liability Company: An Operating Manual* (Nolo). This book can give you a deeper understanding of how to manage your LLC on an ongoing basis, and contains minutes forms as well as resolution forms for recording tax, legal, and management decisions.

# Electing Corporate Tax Treatment

In 1997, the IRS issued new business tax classification rules. Because of these rules, an unincorporated business such as an LLC or a partnership can choose corporate tax treatment without actually incorporating. An LLC can file a simple form with the IRS to receive corporate, rather than pass-through, tax treatment. And make no mistake, these rules mark a groundbreaking event—never before have small businesses been given this kind of tax flexibility by the IRS.

## Corporate Taxation and Income Splitting

First, I want to review how corporations can benefit from corporate tax treatment. Next, I will explain why some LLC owners might want to elect it. Finally, I'll show you how to make the election.

As I mentioned above, unlike a sole proprietorship, a partnership, or an LLC, a corporation starts out as a separate taxable entity. Corporate owners who also work as employees of the corporation pay income taxes on their salary (and any bonuses) on their individual income tax returns. These amounts are tax-deductible to the corporation as business expenses. The corporation itself pays corporate income taxes on any net profits left in the business—that is, on profits that are not paid out to the owners in the form of salary (or bonuses) and are not otherwise deductible to the corporation. If all corporate net income is paid out in the form of salaries, bonuses, and other deductible business expenses, there is no corporate tax due. As you now know, this type of income tax treatment is different from the pass-through tax treatment that LLCs and partnerships start out with, by which unincorporated business owners pay individual income taxes on all net business profits each year, whether or not any profits are distributed to them.

Corporate tax treatment can sometimes lower a business owner's overall tax bill because, for corporate income up to $75,000, the tax rates are only 15% and 25%. These are often lower than the rates individual owners pay on the profits that are passed through to them, which get taxed at their top (marginal) tax rate (assuming the business owner reports taxable income in addition to income from the business).

| Tax Rates on Taxable Corporate Income | |
|---|---|
| $0 to $50,000 | 15% |
| $50,001 to $75,000 | 25% |
| $75,001 to $100,000 | 34% |
| $100,001 to $335,000 | 39% |
| $335,001 to $10,000,000 | 34% |
| $10,000,001 to $15,000,000 | 35% |
| $15,000,001 to $18,333,333 | 38% |
| Over $18,333,333 | 35% |

Note: Personal service corporations are subject to a flat tax of 35% regardless of how much (or how little) they earn.

Owners of a business that will retain some profits in the business from one year to the next can usually save taxes by choosing to be taxed as a corporation. This technique of retaining some profits in the business to be taxed at corporate tax rates while also paying owners salaries and bonuses is called "income splitting."

## Income Splitting in an LLC

As a practical matter, most new LLCs don't elect corporate tax treatment until their LLC is able to pay its owners reasonable salaries. And then they do so only if their tax adviser agrees that the income tax savings that can be achieved by splitting income between the owners and the business are worth the trouble and the collateral tax costs of electing corporate tax treatment.

But for those businesses profitable enough to retain profits in the business from one year to the next, income splitting can result in tax savings. If you run such a business, ask your tax adviser whether corporate tax treatment would save you money.

## How to Elect Corporate Tax Treatment

If you form an LLC and decide that you want your LLC to be taxed like a corporation, you must file IRS Form 8832, *Entity Classification Election*, with the IRS. You simply check the correct box on the form to elect corporate tax treatment—this is the box on the line that reads, "A domestic eligible entity electing to be classified as an association taxable as a corporation." All owners of the business must sign the form, or they must authorize one person to sign it (for example, by signing a simple statement, which is later placed in the LLC records binder, that explicitly authorizes a particular member to sign the form).

RESOURCE
**Online tax forms.** You can get the tax form mentioned above from the IRS website. Go to www.irs.gov and click the link for Forms & Publications, then Current Forms & Pubs. Search for "Form 8832." You can print a blank form to fill in by hand or typewriter, or even better, you can view a "Fill-in Form," insert your information, and print it out.

The tax election takes effect on the date you specify on Form 8832, which must be no more than 75 days before, or 12 months after, you file the form. If you don't specify a date, the tax election will take effect on the date the form is filed with the IRS. The LLC must attach a copy of Form 8832 to its corporate tax return filed during the first tax year when the election is effective.

If your LLC makes the corporate tax election, it should use a double-entry accounting system, start filing corporate income tax returns, and pay estimated corporate income taxes.

> CAUTION
> **Choosing corporate tax status is a tax, not a legal, election.** Even if you elect corporate income tax treatment, your LLC will not be treated like a corporation for any purpose other than paying taxes. You won't have to suddenly appoint a board of directors or issue corporate stock; you are still an LLC, governed by your state's LLC laws. Plus, you still must file annual LLC statements (if required by your LLC filing office) and possibly pay an annual state LLC fee.

## Changing Your Corporate Tax Election

A corporate tax election made with IRS Form 8832 stays in effect until you file another election asking to return to pass-through treatment. However, once a business makes a corporate tax election, it normally cannot change its tax status back to pass-through treatment for at least five years. That's why a business should make a profits projection not only for the current year, but also for future years, before electing corporate treatment. Typically, it makes sense to elect corporate tax status only if it looks like your business will remain solidly profitable for at least several years.

There is, however, one exception to the five-year rule: If more than 50% of the ownership interests in the business change hands after the effective date of the tax election, you can ask the IRS to change your tax status. You do this by submitting a "private letter ruling request," explaining your situation and asking the IRS to allow you to be taxed as a pass-through entity. You'll have to pay the IRS for the privilege, plus pay a tax adviser to help you prepare the request, but it may be worth it if your profits picture changes substantially with a change in ownership.

## Other Issues to Consider

If you and your tax adviser figure out that electing corporate tax treatment will save you enough income tax dollars to be worth a close look, you will want to review other issues before filing your election form. Here are a few things to consider:

- LLC owners who work in the LLC will become corporate employees, subject to payroll taxes. If your LLC already employs workers, this should be no big deal.
- A conversion to corporate tax treatment should be tax-free under Internal Revenue Code Section 351 as long as the LLC owners are "in control" of the company after the conversion. Most actively managed LLCs should meet these technical requirements, but talk to your tax adviser to make sure you will qualify.
- Corporate capital gains tax treatment, corporate loss carryover treatment, and other technical corporate tax provisions are different from the rules that apply to pass-through LLCs. For example, corporations often must pay double taxes when they are liquidated. Also, corporations typically can't pass tax losses through to owners—these losses normally stay with the corporation. You will want to thoroughly review these issues with a knowledgeable tax adviser before electing corporate income tax status.

# LLC Owners and Self-Employment Taxes

If you are an active owner in your LLC (that is, you manage or work for it), your tax adviser will probably recommend that you pay self-employment (Social Security and Medicare) taxes on any profits paid to you. Inactive owners—nonmanaging members in a manager-managed LLC—probably will not have to pay self-employment taxes.

This isn't a big deal for most LLC owners. After all, it's the same way sole proprietors and general partners are treated under the current federal tax system.

On the other hand, limited partners and S corporation shareholders don't have to pay self-employment taxes on their allocated profits (money they receive over and above their salaries). You may wonder why active LLC owners are treated differently. This question has been asked by scores of commentators since the creation of the LLC. And many proposals have been made that would place all owners of limited liability enterprises—S corporations, LLCs, and limited partnerships—on an equal footing. But as of this writing these proposals haven't been adopted. For now, active LLC owners probably have to pay self-employment taxes on all money they receive, but owners of S corporations don't. Check with your tax adviser to determine your self-employment tax strategy.

## An LLC Can Elect to Be Treated as an S Corporation

An LLC can elect S corporation taxation rather than partnership-style pass-through taxation or C corporation taxation. Some active business owners decide to change their LLC into an S corporation in an attempt to save money on self-employment taxes, since an active S corporation business owner is normally not liable for self-employment tax on earnings allocated to the owner.

Under Treasury Regulations Sec. 301.7701-3(c)(1)(v)(C), if an LLC files a valid S corporation tax election (using IRS Form 2553), the IRS will assume that the LLC first filed an election to have the LLC treated as a corporation (normally, this is done by filing IRS Form 8832) and then filed the S corporation tax election (Form 2553).

Note that this is an aggressive tax strategy and is by no means the standard way of organizing an LLC. Please elect S corporation taxation for your LLC only after talking with an experienced tax adviser who knows the rules for and the consequences of turning your LLC into an S corporation.

# LLC Management

In every business, at least one person needs to be in charge of the overall management of the business, and the LLC is no exception. Under most states' legal rules, all LLC members are automatically equally responsible for managing the LLC. For example, in an LLC that has four members, all four are its business managers. In LLC legal jargon, this arrangement is called "member management." But there is another possible LLC management approach—manager management—by which LLC members can choose one or more members and/or nonmembers to manage their LLC. In most states, you must specify whether your LLC is member- or manager-managed in the organizational paperwork (your LLC articles or certificate) you file with the LLC filing office.

## Member Versus Manager Management

Here's an overview of each type of LLC management, and examples of businesses for which each management structure might be appropriate.

### Member Management

The owners of most smaller LLCs choose the standard member management approach, in which all LLC members are responsible for managing the LLC. (A few states call the managers "governors.") This approach makes sense because, in most smaller LLCs, all members plan to be active in the business, and all want to be able to vote on how the LLC will be run.

> **EXAMPLE:** James and Amy form Tree Trimmers, LLC, a landscaping business. Amy transfers title to her Ford Ranchero pickup to the LLC to help with hauling, and James contributes cash equal to the truck's value. Both want to manage the LLC, so they select member management in their articles of organization.

## Manager Management

Member management, however, isn't the best choice for all LLCs. Under the other management option—manager management—an LLC is managed by a single manager or a small group of managers consisting of:

- one or more selected LLC members
- one or more nonmembers (usually either officers or outside investors), or
- a mixture of the two.

Choosing manager management instead of member management might make sense if you're planning to bring in outside investors who do not want to take a management role in your business.

> EXAMPLE 1: Let's continue with Tree Trimmers, LLC. Even before James and Amy open the doors to their new landscaping business, they immediately sign up more customers than they can handle. Amy and James realize that they'll need extra cash up front to buy a second pickup truck so that each can go out on separate landscape jobs. A friend of theirs, Antonio, agrees to put up the necessary cash to buy the second truck, in exchange for a proportionate capital interest in the new LLC. A busy programmer with no interest in landscape gardening, Antonio does not want to work for or run the LLC. As a result, James and Amy form a manager-managed LLC, with themselves as the two managers. Antonio is simply a nonmanaging member.

> EXAMPLE 2: Jason is an electronics engineer who works for a design company. A coworker, Jamal, is a highly skilled engineer who wants to quit his day job and strike out on his own, doing custom electronics design for client companies. Jason has some extra cash on hand and agrees to invest in Jamal's new LLC. Jamal will manage and work in the new business full time, and Jason will merely invest in it and do occasional design jobs for a fee. The new LLC is managed by Jamal only, and Jason becomes a nonmanaging member.

Manager management also may make sense for an LLC in these situations:

- The LLC owners decide to hire a chief executive who is more qualified or otherwise better suited to manage the LLC than the current LLC members.
- The LLC wishes to give an outsider (a nonmember) a vote in management. For instance, an outsider might be willing to lend money to the LLC only in exchange for a say in management decisions. To give the nonmember management authority, the LLC must select manager management and create a management group that includes the outsider.
- The sole member of an LLC wants to manage the business but gives membership interests to nonmanaging family members who will step into a management role only when the current owner-manager steps down.

As these examples indicate, the people you select as managers do not need to be owners of the LLC. You can select LLC officers and executives or anyone else you wish as a manager.

Fortunately, an LLC can easily choose manager management to handle any of these situations. You just select manager management in your articles (most states require you to specify your management structure this way) or in your operating agreement (required in the other states). In all states, just one manager is required to manage a manager-managed LLC, but there is no upper limit to the number of managers you can have.

In most small LLCs, managers serve for an indefinite term—that is, until the members of the LLC vote to replace or remove them. Typically, LLC operating agreements allow an LLC manager to be removed or replaced for any or no particular reason upon the vote of the full membership (nonmanaging members as well as managing members). In other words, state law lets LLC members decide for themselves when managers can be removed. Some larger LLCs, however, prefer to have managers serve for a definite term, such as one year, at the end of which the members reelect or replace the managers. This procedure is usually used only in more formal LLCs with at least several outside investors who are nonmanaging members. That's because, unlike corporations, where shareholders reelect or replace the board of directors each year, most LLCs choose not to require a periodic review and election of managers, unless they have outside investors who demand it. In fact, most LLCs pick an initial management team and stick with it for the long term, unless there is a problem and one or more managers need to be replaced.

TIP
**Manager management will not affect limited liability.** In a manager-managed LLC, all members, managing or not, get to keep their personal liability protection. This is a fundamentally different approach than the liability protection that applies to limited partnerships, where at least one general partner must be personally liable for partnership debts and liabilities.

If you decide to choose managers, it's important to realize that state law still leaves certain voting rights in the hands of the nonmanaging members. As just mentioned, LLC members have the right to remove and replace managers. Also, nonmanaging members have the right to approve fundamental changes to the LLC and its membership, including (in many states) the power to amend the articles or operating agreement of the LLC, to merge or dissolve the LLC, to approve or deny the admission of new members, and to approve or deny the transfer of an LLC membership from an existing member to an outsider.

CAUTION
**Securities law consequence of manager management.** If you choose manager management, ownership interests in your LLC may be classified as securities because nonmanaging members may be investing their money in a business in which they're not actively participating. Instead, they expect to make money from the efforts of others. This type of investment is classified as a security—see Chapter 6 for more information.

# Legal Authority of LLC Members and Managers

Any member of a member-managed LLC, or any manager of a manager-managed LLC, can legally bind the LLC to a contract or business transaction. In other words, each of these people is an agent of the LLC, and can singlehandedly commit the entire LLC to a contract or business deal. This is the same legal authority given each partner in a general partnership.

There are some exceptions to the legal authority of LLC members and managers. An LLC usually can't be held to a contract or deal if it was clearly outside the normal course of LLC business, or if the outsider contracting with the member or manager knew that the LLC member or manager did not have specific authority to conduct that transaction. For example, if a member of an LLC that operates a small local fish store tries to commit the LLC to purchasing a TV station, the sellers would be well advised to make sure that member really has the authority to do the deal. If they didn't check and a court fight followed, a judge would probably find that because TV stations and fish stores are completely unrelated, the ambitious LLC member had no legal authority to bind the LLC. In that case, the member might be held personally to the contract, but the LLC would not be bound to carry it out. Unfortunately, when it comes to trying to disavow the actions of rogue LLC members or managers in less extreme situations, lack of authority can be hard to prove.

> **EXAMPLE:** Gary is a member and VP of Fish and Fritters Fast Foods LLC, a member-managed LLC. He orders $5,000 of goods from Joe's Office Supply Company, a local merchant, consisting of $4,000 of LLC stationery and routine office supplies plus $1,000 of personal letterhead and an expensive pen with his name embossed on it. When he places the order, he does so on behalf of his LLC, and charges the bill to his LLC's account. Joe, the owner of the office supply company, gets a check from the LLC for $4,000, with a note from the LLC accounts payable officer advising Joe to collect the $1,000 balance from Gary, because the

order for personal letterhead and the pen had nothing to do with the LLC. Would a small claims court let Joe recover the $1,000 balance from the LLC itself? Yes. Joe would normally be justified in believing that a member of the LLC had authority to place the full order on behalf of the LLC.

The moral should be clear. Local fish markets trying to buy TV stations aside, it's always safest to assume that your LLC will be legally bound by any contract or transaction signed or entered into on behalf of your LLC by any member or manager, no matter how unreasonable the deal is. This broad legal authority should not present a problem if you choose the right people to be members or managers of your LLC in the first place. But it can be poison if you work with the wrong people. If you're uncomfortable with the idea of a particular co-owner having the authority to obligate your entire business, you shouldn't go into business with that person. And if you don't like the fact that any co-owner can bind your business to any deal, a multi-owner LLC is probably not the right type of business for you. Instead, you may want to form a one-owner LLC, where you are completely in charge.

## Member and Manager Meetings

Before looking at the basic rules for holding LLC meetings, I want to make one point clear: routine LLC business decisions—whether the LLC is managed by members or managers—are made without holding formal LLC meetings, recording votes in written minutes, or signing written consent forms. (See Chapter 6 for more on minutes and consent forms.)

> EXAMPLE: Xenon X-Ray Systems, a medical electronics LLC, decides to increase inventory in anticipation of a surge of upcoming orders. The decision is made by the VP of Manufacturing, after getting a nod of approval from the CEO. A formal LLC meeting, documented by written minutes, is not held, nor do the LLC's managers or members sign written consent forms.

Major items of LLC business are often discussed and voted on in formal member or manager meetings, however. "Major" items are usually those that affect the basic structure of the company, including the removal of managers, the admission of a new member, the transfer of a membership interest, the amendment of the operating agreement, and the sale of all or most of the assets of the LLC. In addition, meetings can be held anytime an LLC member or officer feels a decision should be formally approved by a full vote. Decisions that might warrant more formality include the approval of a large LLC bank loan, the purchase of LLC real estate, the expansion of the LLC product line, or the acquisition of a new business venture by the LLC.

Most states do not have rules dictating when and how formal LLC meetings should take place. Several states do, but, as is usual in most areas of LLC law, these rules apply only if you don't set out your own rules in your operating agreement. Either way, you should obviously spell out in your LLC operating agreement who can call meetings, how notice of a meeting should be given, and how many participants must be present for a valid meeting to take place, as well as the basic rules for conducting a meeting. If you don't create sensible procedural rules for your LLC, you may have to follow the rules set out in your state's LLC statutes.

That said, your LLC operating agreement does not have to require that particular meetings be held at particular times during the year (required meetings of this sort are called "regular" or "annual" meetings). Instead, it can simply set up procedures to allow any LLC member or manager to call a "special meeting" when the need arises—typically, when an important legal, business, or tax decision needs to be made. Does this mean that LLCs never hold annual meetings? No. It just means that LLC operating agreements rarely require that such meetings be held. In fact, LLCs with investors who are not involved in the business often do call a meeting at the end of each year to keep the nonmanaging investors aware of how well management is meeting the LLC's financial goals and what the financial objectives are for the upcoming year.

EXAMPLE: Castoff Clothing, LLC, started as a clothing wholesaler that supplied used designer clothes to antique clothing boutiques. Business boomed, and an investment company with 12 individual owners (called Pinnacle Investments) bought a one-third interest in Castoff. After the investment, Castoff changed from member management to manager management and added a seat on its management team for the Pinnacle CEO. Since the changeover, Castoff has held biannual management meetings to which all Pinnacle investors are invited. This annual meeting keeps the investment group fully informed on how Castoff is doing, keeping the lines of communication open between the partnered companies.

Again, in smaller LLCs without a broad investor base, annual meetings of this sort are less common. Instead, special meetings are called when an important item of business needs to be formally approved or the issue at hand is controversial, making it sensible to hold face-to-face discussions that will be recorded with written minutes. Here are a few examples of scenarios that may warrant a special meeting in a smaller LLC:

- An important legal or tax formality needs to be approved and recorded. For example, your LLC is admitting a new member or approving the buy-back of a departing member's interest in the LLC.

- You need to meet face-to-face with your full membership—including any less active investors—and formally approve an out-of-the-ordinary or important business decision. For example, if the LLC will sell important LLC assets or purchase real estate, the decision should be approved at a formal meeting and recorded in the minutes.

- A controversial business decision needs to be discussed or a dispute resolved; for example, some members of your LLC want to dissolve or sell the business and others don't, or one member wants to acquire a new product line that another thinks is a terrible investment. Holding a formal meeting prevents later claims that a decision was made secretly or without disclosure of all key facts.

- A member has a conflict of interest in an upcoming deal that the LLC is considering. For example, if a member is proposing a business deal for the LLC that will personally benefit him or her more than the other members, a frank discussion where the member discloses how he or she will profit from the deal, complete with minutes, is clearly in order.

- In a manager-managed LLC, you need to reelect managers to another term (assuming managers serve for a fixed term). For example, if you adopt a two-year term for your managers in your operating agreement, you will want to hold membership meetings every second year to reelect your managers.

**RESOURCE**

**More information on holding meetings and recording decisions.**
For practical information on calling and holding LLC meetings, see my book, *Your Limited Liability Company: An Operating Manual* (Nolo). This practical manual also contains all of the ready-to-use minutes forms and consent forms you need to formally approve ongoing LLC decisions and document them for your LLC records binder, as well as resolutions for the various decisions LLC members can make.

## Member and Manager Voting Rights

Your operating agreement should specify how much voting power each member or manager gets to exercise at a member or manager meeting. If it doesn't, your state's statutory rules will determine how your members and managers vote. In most states, the law requires LLC member voting rights to be allocated according to the members' capital (ownership) interests, unless you provide otherwise in your articles or operating agreement. For example, a member contributing 50% of the capital to the LLC gets 50% of the voting power of the LLC unless there is an agreement providing otherwise. However, in some states, the default voting rule is that, absent an agreement, members are given voting rights on a per capita basis (one vote per member).

Most LLCs want to mete out votes in proportion to the members' contributions of capital. After all, the level of each member's risk for poor management decisions can be measured by the amount each invests in the LLC— that's what each member has to lose. But in special circumstances, you may decide instead that a per capita rule (one vote per member) better reflects the way the business works.

> **EXAMPLE:** Dorothy and Frances start Bungee Jump Adventures LLC. Dorothy contributes most of the start-up capital for a 90% capital interest, while Frances adds a bit of cash for a 10% share. Frances will be the jump operator, who often will strap herself in for dual drops with novice jumpers. Aside from purchasing reliable bungee gear and paying for a telephone answering service to take calls from clients, initial expenses are minimal. In their LLC operating agreement, Frances insists on equal voting power, reasoning that although she has only a 10% capital stake in the enterprise, her personal risk of life and limb should qualify her for a 50% share in important management decisions.

No matter how voting power is allocated among members, under state statutory rules, most LLC matters brought to a vote of the members must be approved by at least a majority of the LLC's voting power. In other words, more than 50% of the full voting interests of the members is required to approve a decision, whether the members have various percentages of voting power or they have one vote each. Some decisions, such as changing the LLC articles or operating agreements, may require unanimous consent.

> **EXAMPLE:** Sit-u-ational Awareness, LLC, a California ergonomics consulting firm, has parceled out its voting interests in its operating agreement according to the capital interests of its three members, as follows: Kathlyn–30%, Evan–25%, and Alyson–45%. The

operating agreement (and the default provisions in California's LLC act) further says that the vote of a majority of LLC voting power is required to decide an issue brought to the membership for resolution. Because of the capital and voting interests of the members, at least two of the three members must agree to approve a membership resolution brought to a vote at a members' meeting.

Of course, your operating agreement can state that a decision must be approved by the vote of a larger majority of the membership. For instance, you can require that any matter brought before the members be approved by two-thirds of the voting interests of the members.

If an LLC is manager managed, state statutory rules typically give managers one vote each if there is more than one manager. And most states' LLC laws also require a majority of the manager votes to approve management decisions. Although LLCs can adopt different manager voting rules (state law usually applies when LLCs fail to state a different rule in their operating agreement), most simply copy the "one manager, one vote" procedure from their state LLC act, believing that it works well.

EXAMPLE: Dollars to Donuts, LLC, which uses the trade name D2D, an emerging franchiser and promoter of the one-buck-per-dozen-donut discount offer on every tenth donut purchase, is owned by four entrepreneurs. But D2D is managed by a team of five managers consisting of the four members and a nonmember pastry chef, Pierre (who brings to the business his secret recipe for the "twissant," a delectable French pastry, plus his formidable baking skills). Their LLC operating agreement says that, on management decisions, each manager gets one vote, and the vote of at least three of the five managers is required to resolve a disputed issue. Far from functioning as a fifth wheel on the management team, Pierre has become the all-important tie-breaking vote should the four owners split their votes.

# Starting and Running Your LLC:
# The Paperwork

I n this chapter, I focus on the basic legal documents you'll use to set up your LLC. Then, I'll review the legal formalities you'll need to follow to organize and operate your LLC, including ongoing record-keeping requirements and necessary government filings. Finally, I'll alert you to an issue that all multi-member LLCs should be aware of: In some circumstances, there's a small chance that federal and state securities agencies could treat membership interests in your LLC as securities (like shares in a publicly traded corporation). I'll explain the issues involved and outline your options if it appears likely that you'll have to comply with any of these securities laws.

## Paperwork Required to Form an LLC

Setting up your own LLC is easy—it should take you relatively little time to turn your idea for an LLC into a legal reality. In most states, one person—called the "LLC organizer"—can prepare and file all of the necessary paperwork on behalf of the other initial members of the LLC.

CAUTION

**Not all professionals can form LLCs.** As I discussed in Chapter 1, California doesn't allow certain professionals to form LLCs (but some may be able to form RLLPs—see Chapter 2). A number of other states require professionals to follow special rules when forming an LLC, including putting profession-specific language in their articles of organization. And in some states, professionals who want to form an LLC must obtain a statement from their state licensing board certifying that they have a current state license, which they must file with the LLC articles. If you have a vocational or professional license, call your state LLC filing office to find out whether you can form an LLC in your state, and if so, whether there are special rules or restrictions.

## Articles of Organization

In most states, the only formal legal step you must take to create an LLC is to prepare and file LLC articles of organization with your state's LLC filing office. (In some states, this organizational document is called a "certificate of organization" or a "certificate of formation.") A few states require you to take an additional step, however: Prior to filing your articles, you must publish your intent to form an LLC in a local newspaper.

The LLC filing office is usually the same one that handles your state's corporate filings, typically the secretary or department of state's office, located in the state's capital city. More populous states often have branch offices in other major cities. Instructions for finding each state's LLC filing office website are in Appendix A, under the heading "Business Entity Filing Office."

Your LLC articles of organization needn't be lengthy or complex. In fact, you may be able to prepare your own by filling in the blanks and checking the boxes on a form provided by your state's LLC filing office. In many states, you can prepare and file your articles online, from the state's filing office website. Typically, you need only specify a few basic details about your LLC, such as its name, the address of its main office, the agent and office you're designating to receive legal papers, and the names of its initial members. Below is an example of LLC articles of organization for a member-run LLC that includes the type of information many states require.

If you're designating a special management team to run the LLC, you'll probably have to list the names of your managers on your articles form.

TIP

**Converting a partnership to an LLC may require a different form.**
Some states require existing partnerships that are converting to an LLC to file a special articles form for their new LLC. This form is often called a "certificate of conversion." Call your state's LLC filing office (or go online to its website) to see if it has a special conversion form. You'll find contact information in Appendix A.

# Articles of Organization
## of
## Luxor Light LLC

The undersigned natural persons, of the age of eighteen years or more, acting as organizers of a limited liability company under the _Anystate_ Limited Liability Company Act, adopt the following Articles of Organization for such limited liability company.

**Article 1. Name of Limited Liability Company.** The name of this limited liability company is _Luxor Light LLC_ .

**Article 2. Registered Office and Registered Agent.** The initial registered office of this limited liability company and the name of its initial registered agent at this address are: _Robert Johnston, 1515 San Estudillo, Anycity, Anystate, 00000_ .

**Article 3. Statement of Purposes.** The purposes for which this limited liability company is organized are: _to operate a custom home and commercial lighting and fixture store, and to engage in any other lawful business for which limited liability companies may be organized in this state._

**Article 4. Management and Names and Addresses of Initial Members.** The management of this limited liability company is reserved to the members. The names and addresses of its initial members are:
_Robert Johnston, 1515 San Estudillo, Anycity, Anystate, 00000_
_Rebecca Johnston, 1515 San Estudillo, Anycity, Anystate, 00000_
_Gregory Luxor, 3021 Los Avenidos, Anycity, Anystate, 00000_

**Article 5. Principal Place of Business of the Limited Liability Company.** The principal place of business of the limited liability company shall be:
_56 Rue de Campanille, Anycity, Anystate, 00000_

**Article 6. Period of Duration of the Limited Liability Company.** The period of duration of the limited liability company shall be: ___perpetual___ .

In Witness Whereof, the undersigned organizer of this limited liability company has signed these Articles of Organization on the date indicated.

Date: ___[date]___

Signature(s): ___*Gregory Luxor*___

Printed Name: ___Gregory Luxor___

Title: ___Organizer___

Your LLC articles will be rejected by the LLC filing office if the proposed name of your LLC is already in use by another LLC, corporation, or other type of registered business in your state. The best way to make sure you don't run into this problem is to check with your state LLC filing office—before you settle on a name and prepare your paperwork—to see whether your proposed name is available. If it is, most states allow you to reserve it for 60 days or more for a small fee. Once you reserve your name, it is guaranteed to be available for your use when you file your LLC articles, as long as you do so within the reservation period. Many states allow you to check name availability online, and they often provide a downloadable reservation form you can use to reserve an available name. Some let you reserve your name online, as well.

Here are some issues to consider when picking a name for your LLC:

- Your proposed business name shouldn't be similar to another business's name or trademark. The LLC filing office will tell you if another LLC in your state is already using your proposed name, but you're on your own as to the names and trademarks of other businesses in your state and in the rest of the country. To be sure another business in your field isn't already using the name or trademark you want to use, you should conduct a trademark search.
- The name should do a good job of marketing your goods and services.
- Your state may require your LLC name to include or end with an LLC designator, such as "Limited Liability Company" or "Limited Company," or an abbreviation of these words, such as "LLC" or "Ltd. Liability Co."
- The name usually can't include words like "banking," "trust," "insurance," or similar terms that refer to financial services businesses.

**RESOURCE**

**Choosing a business name.** My primary goal in this section is to alert you to the steps you'll need to take to form an LLC in your state, so I don't explore a number of potentially complicated and important legal issues that can come into play when you choose and use a business name. To learn more about trademark law, get a copy of *Trademark: Legal Care for Your Business & Product Name*, by Stephen Elias and Richard Stim (Nolo). In addition to educating you about trademark law, this book will help you choose a strong marketing name and search for possibly conflicting trademarks.

**RESOURCE**

**Protecting your business name.** Once you have chosen a business name and filed your articles of organization, you may wish to take extra steps to protect it. If you will be using the name to sell goods or services, you may wish to register it as a trademark with your state and the U.S. Patent and Trademark Office. The application procedures are relatively simple and reasonably inexpensive, and are fully explained in *Trademark: Legal Care for Your Business & Product Name*, by Stephen Elias and Richard Stim (Nolo).

## Operating Agreement

Even though operating agreements need not be filed with the LLC filing office and are not explicitly required in most states, every LLC should create a written operating agreement to define the basic rights and responsibilities of members and managers. An LLC operating agreement sets out membership rights such as the members' capital (ownership) interests and distributive shares (the profits that will be allocated to the members). An operating agreement should also specify whether any actual distributions of profits must be made to the members or whether the LLC can retain all of the profits in the business—see Chapter 3 for a review of the difference between distributive shares and actual distributions. How the LLC will be managed and the voting power of members and managers is also covered in the operating agreement, as well as housekeeping details like rules for holding meetings and taking votes. Lastly, an operating agreement should contain buy-out provisions (unless the LLC will have a separate buy-out agreement), which explain what will happen if a member wants to sell his or her interest, dies, or becomes disabled.

What happens if you don't prepare an operating agreement and you later run into a serious conflict with other members? Your LLC's legal life will be controlled by your state's LLC statutes. This means that state law, not the choices you and your business associates make, will dictate how the dispute is resolved. For example, many states have a default rule that LLC profits and losses must be divided up among the members equally, regardless of each member's capital contribution. Is this really how you would split up profits in your LLC, even if one of your members invests twice as much as the others? If not, you have to adopt a different rule in your operating agreement.

> **EXAMPLE:** Yvonne and Joe form an LLC with Yvonne contributing 30% of the capital and Joe contributing 70%. Under their state's default rule, Yvonne and Joe would each be entitled to one-half the profits of the LLC each year, even though they paid unequal amounts to get the LLC started. But if Yvonne and Joe prepare their own operating agreement, they can agree to divide profits according to their capital contribution percentages, or any other way they wish. (See Chapter 3 for more on special allocations.)

For reasons like this, I believe it's a big mistake to run an LLC without an operating agreement. Without an agreement defining the rights and responsibilities of members, you won't control the answers to basic questions like these:

- When your members are faced with an important management decision, does each get one vote, or do they vote according to their LLC capital interests or profits interests (distributive shares)?

How many members make up a quorum (the minimum number of members who must be present before a vote is taken)? If your LLC has managers, does each manager get one vote? And how many managers make up a quorum?

- What if a member wants to increase his or her capital interest percentage? Can other members refuse to allow it, or will their relative capital percentages decrease if they decide not to match the additional investment?

- How much—if any—of the allocated profits of the LLC must be distributed to LLC members each year? Can members at least expect their LLC to pay them enough to cover the income taxes they'll owe on each year's allocations of LLC profits? (Members are allocated and taxed on profits each year, whether or not any profits are actually paid to them, as explained in Chapter 4.)

- Does your LLC have to hold an annual membership meeting? Who can call special meetings of the membership during the year? What are the procedures for giving notice of a special meeting to the LLC members?

- If your LLC needs additional operating capital after it gets started, are the owners expected to invest more money in the business?

- Can a member leave the LLC at any time? If so, is the LLC, or are its members, required to buy back the departing member's interest? What if they can't agree on a fair price?

- Is a departing member allowed to sell an interest to an outsider? If so, can the remaining members stop the sale or refuse to admit the purchaser as a new, voting member?

These kinds of questions can, and frequently do, come back to haunt small business owners, particularly if they have a falling out and haven't written down the details of their agreement. You can almost guarantee that in times of tension everyone will remember these details differently. The best strategy is to discuss these and other key issues at the beginning of your venture and record these points in a written operating agreement. That way, you can get on with LLC business without having to worry too much about future changes or disputes.

> **RELATED TOPIC**
>
> **Sample operating agreement.** Appendix B contains a sample operating agreement for a member-run LLC that is typical of one commonly used in many states. However, the laws do vary from state to state, so don't model your operating agreement on our sample alone.

## Filing a Fictitious or Assumed Business Name

The remaining items in this section cover the legal formalities necessary to perfect the organization of your LLC. The first one I'll turn to is selecting an assumed or fictitious business name for your LLC.

Many LLCs will operate under their formal LLC name—the name they put in their articles of organization. For example, a computer repair shop might file its articles under the name Fix Me LLC and also do business under that name. In that case, the LLC doesn't have to file its business name anywhere. But some LLC owners like to operate their LLC under a name that's different from the formal name listed in their articles of organization.

> **EXAMPLE:** The owners of Solar Plexus Flex and Fitness Center Ltd. Liability Co. decide to operate their fitness centers under the fictitious name "Flextime Fitness Center." The LLC owners don't want to change their formal LLC name as stated in their articles of organization; they just think that name is a bit long for marketing purposes.

Fortunately, you should have no problem operating your business under a different name than the one you used to organize your LLC. To do this, most states simply require your LLC to file a "fictitious" or "assumed" business name statement (this name is often called a "DBA"—short for "doing business as") and pay a small fee. The purpose of this filing is to allow vendors, creditors, and customers who encounter your fictitious name to track down the real owners of your business. You normally file this paperwork with the secretary of state's office or the local county clerk's office. In some states, both a state and county filing are required. Find out your state's rules by calling your LLC filing office or going to its website.

Some states also require you to publish your intent to use a fictitious name in a local newspaper at least once. Newspapers with legal notice classified sections will make the required publications for a modest fee and file an affidavit of publication with the state or local county clerk. Calling a local newspaper is generally the easiest way to discover whether your state requires the publication of a fictitious or assumed name statement and how to satisfy any related state requirements.

**RESOURCE**

**Small business legal resources.** Nolo's website, www.nolo.com, contains lots of free, helpful information on other start-up steps that apply to all businesses, not just the particular steps that apply to forming an LLC. For instance, you'll find information on writing a business plan, choosing a business name, selecting a business location, arranging for financing, and setting up bookkeeping and accounting systems.

## Additional Steps for Existing Businesses

**SKIP AHEAD**

These extra steps apply only to owners of existing businesses. If your business is a start-up—that is, you are not converting a sole proprietorship or a partnership to an LLC—you can safely skip this section. Go to "Ongoing LLC Paperwork," below.

If you're converting an existing business to an LLC, you'll need to notify the IRS, your state taxing authority, and other governmental agencies that you've changed your business's legal status to an LLC, and you'll need to give them your new LLC name. As part of this process, you will need to transfer ID numbers, licenses, and permits to your new LLC name, including:

- your federal Employer Identification Number (EIN) (a multi-member LLC must have its own EIN)
- your state employer identification number
- your sales tax permit
- your business license
- your professional licenses or permits, if applicable, and
- your fictitious or assumed business name statement (this applies only if you'll operate your LLC under a name other than its formal name, as explained above).

Of course, you'll also want to change your stationery, business cards, brochures, advertisements, signs, and other marketing and business miscellany to reflect your new LLC status and name. In addition, you'll want to let your suppliers, customers, business associates, and bank know your new business name and LLC status. You can do this simply by sending a letter to each company on your new LLC letterhead stationery, telling them that you converted your business to an LLC.

> **TIP**
>
> **Review your files and other papers for more contacts.** If you go through your lists of customers, suppliers, professional directories, and the like, you'll surely discover the names and addresses of other agencies and businesses that should be told of your conversion. Add them to your list.

## Terminating a Prior Partnership

If you're converting a partnership to an LLC, you may need to do a little extra paperwork to end the partnership's legal existence.

General partnerships normally don't file organizational papers with the state to get started, so if you are converting a general partnership to an LLC, you won't need to file a document with the state to terminate your partnership. But some states require you to publish a "notice of dissolution of partnership" in a local newspaper. If you don't, a creditor of the partnership could sue the owners of the new LLC personally for unpaid debts, because the creditor wasn't aware that the partnership ended. Any newspaper that handles legal filings should be able to explain your state's rules. Once you publish your notice, the newspaper should send you a copy of the published notice and an affidavit of publication to place in your files.

Limited partnerships—which have to make an initial filing with the state to create their partnership entity—must also file a document letting the state know that the partnership no longer exists. If your state provides a special form to convert a partnership to an LLC (often called a certificate of conversion), however, your partnership should be automatically terminated when you file this form—there should be no need to file anything else. If your state does not provide a special articles form to convert your partnership to an LLC, you may need to terminate the partnership yourself. To do this, you'll probably file a "certificate of termination," or similarly titled document, with the state agency where you filed your original limited partnership papers. To find out exactly what's required, call your state LLC filing office or browse its website for instructions on how to terminate a partnership.

### If Your Prior Business Owed Money

If you are converting a sole proprietorship or partnership to an LLC, and the prior business has outstanding claims or debts, you and your co-owners will remain personally liable for these debts. Of course, this should not be a problem if your new LLC plans to assume and pay these bills as they come due. But as a courtesy, and to make sure all creditors of the prior business have notice of your new business form, you should send a letter to notify creditors that you're converting your prior business to an LLC, and ask them to put future bills in the name of your LLC. If your prior business has significant disputed debts or claims that your LLC will not automatically pay when it begins doing business, I strongly urge you to talk to a business lawyer about your legal responsibilities and rights as to these disputed amounts, and whether you'll have to take any extra steps when converting your business to an LLC.

In a few states, some types of businesses that convert to an LLC are required to comply with what is known as the "bulk sales law." This law may apply when retail, wholesale, manufacturing, and restaurant businesses convert to a new legal form. This law requires the publication of various notices in a local newspaper, plus a waiting period before the conversion takes place, to allow creditors of the prior business to submit claims for unpaid bills. These requirements are meant to make it more difficult for the owners of a business that owes money to change its business form—usually to one with limited liability protection—without arranging to take care of its past debts. However, even if you are converting a business that is subject to the bulk sales law, you may be able to exempt yourself from most of the law's notice requirements and waiting periods by agreeing to assume the debts and liabilities of the prior business.

> **SEE AN EXPERT**
>
> **Get help with your state's bulk sales rules.** A local newspaper that publishes legal notices can help you understand and meet your state's bulk sales requirements. Normally the publication requirements are not onerous, and the fees are small. If you have lots of debts—especially if some are disputed—ask a local small business lawyer how to proceed. Trying to figure out every nuance of these laws yourself simply won't be worth your time.

# Ongoing LLC Paperwork

Let's now take a look at the ongoing legal formalities an LLC should follow. Fortunately, LLCs aren't required to generate a lot of paperwork, but you will need to create some basic records and file necessary annual forms.

## Maintaining a Records Binder

You will want to keep your important LLC documents, such as your articles or certificate of organization, LLC operating agreement, minutes of members' meetings (and managers' meetings, if applicable), leases, major contracts, and the like in a safe, convenient place. I recommend setting up an organized system for maintaining these LLC records, whether in manila envelopes, file folders, or a more expensive LLC records binder. You aren't legally required to use a separate records binder, but many LLCs decide to go this more formal route, if only to remind themselves to take their record keeping seriously.

## Written Records of Important Decisions

It's a good idea to document all important business decisions that require member or manager approval. Although LLCs can conduct business less formally than corporations, it is nevertheless wise to document and record your major business decisions. In a worst-case scenario, if an LLC keeps few or no records, a court might disregard the LLC's legal existence and hold its members personally liable for business debts (see Chapter 1). Formally documenting key LLC actions is also a good way to keep any members who are not involved in the day-to-day management of your LLC fully informed of major LLC decisions.

An even more important reason to document key LLC decisions is to reduce the possibility of future controversy and dissension among LLC members. Even in the ranks of a small LLC where all of the members are friends, this is likely to occur if key decisions are not recorded. The 13th-century legal scholar, Beaumanoir, made this point beautifully in his *Coutumes de Beauvaisis*: "For the memory of men slips and flows away, and the life of man is short, and that which is not written is soon forgotten."

The following are some examples of LLC decisions that should be recorded:

- a vote to change (amend) the LLC articles or operating agreement
- a vote on matters that require a member or manager vote, as set out in the LLC's operating agreement; typically, these matters include admitting a new member to the LLC, buying back a member's interest in the LLC, and dissolving the LLC
- a vote to make significant capital outlays—to purchase real property, for example; banks and escrow and title companies often ask LLCs to submit a copy of written minutes or a written consent approving this type of transaction

- a vote to sell real estate or other major LLC assets; again, escrow and title companies, as well as buyers, will ask for paperwork approving this kind of transaction
- a decision to fund a major or significant recurring LLC expense, such as contributions to an employee pension or profit-sharing plan, or to authorize a significant loan or line of credit
- a vote to make significant state or federal tax elections (such as electing corporate tax treatment)
- a decision to expand or discontinue a line of products or services
- a decision to pursue or settle a lawsuit, and
- approvals of other important legal, business, financial, or tax decisions.

CAUTION

**State law may require unanimous or majority consent for some decisions.** Your state's LLC act may require the consent of all or a majority of the LLC's members for a few types of fundamental decisions, regardless of what your operating agreement says. Such decisions might include an amendment to the LLC articles or operating agreement, the departure of a member, the transfer of a membership to an outsider, or the approval of the admission of a new member.

Many of these decisions are made at LLC meetings—either an annual meeting (if you provide for one) or a special meeting called by the members during the year. (Chapter 5 covers annual and special meetings.) After each meeting, minutes that state the business discussed and approved at the meeting should be prepared—in plain English, not legalese. A copy of the minutes should be placed, together with any notices of the meeting and documents or reports presented at the meeting, in the LLC records binder.

Many one- and two-person LLCs will not want to hold a meeting every time they have to make a major LLC decision. Of course, holding a meeting with yourself is a bit silly. But even when meetings aren't necessary, it makes sense to keep good records of important decisions. That's why most states allow LLC members to record important decisions on written consent forms—documents that state what was decided and are signed by all members at the bottom to show their consent.

> **CAUTION**
> **A resource for ongoing paperwork.** The legal formalities involved in operating an LLC are not difficult. I provide step-by-step instructions for handling these tasks in *Your Limited Liability Company: An Operating Manual* (Nolo). You may want to take a look at this practical guide, which contains minutes and consent forms you can use to formally approve ongoing LLC decisions, as well as resolutions for the various decisions LLC members can make.

The good news is that you don't need to document routine business decisions—only those that require manager or member approval. You don't have to clutter up your LLC record binder with paperwork showing that you bought supplies or products, hired or fired employees, launched new services or products, or other standard business decisions.

## Annual Report Filings

Most states require an LLC to file a short annual report form with the same state filing office where your articles of organization were filed— typically the secretary or department of state's office. The LLC filing office mails out these forms to LLCs every year. These forms typically require basic biographical information, such as the names and addresses of current LLC members and/or managers and the name and address of the LLC's registered agent and office for service of legal process. In some states, you can leave items blank if there is no change in the information from the previous annual report filing. Most states require you to pay a small fee, usually in the $10 to $50 range, with this form, but annual fees in a few states may be higher.

## Proof of LLC Status

Before doing business with your LLC, such as entering into a contract, signing a lease, or agreeing to sell or buy property, financial institutions, trade creditors, or other businesses may want to see formal legal paperwork that establishes the existence of your LLC. This is particularly likely if you apply to borrow money, purchase securities, or buy or sell real estate. You can normally satisfy lenders and potential business partners by providing a copy of your articles of organization. But occasionally, you may be required to purchase a certified copy of your LLC articles of organization to show others. This form should be available for a small fee from your state LLC filing office. It should be officially file-stamped by that office, and may also contain formal language stating that your LLC has met all necessary state formalities to begin doing business in your state. A few even come with an embossed gold seal!

Once in a while, you'll find some outsiders who are such sticklers for detail that they insist you prove your legal status on the date they are dealing with you. After all, your articles of organization only show that you met the state's legal requirements when you originally formed your LLC—not that your legal status is currently valid. Most states will help you satisfy requests for current information by allowing you to obtain, for a small fee, a certificate of good standing, showing that your LLC meets all state legal and tax requirements on the date of your status request. This should satisfy even the most cautious outsider that your LLC is a bona fide legal entity.

## Income Tax Filings

Now let's look at the most common tax paperwork that's used during the life of an LLC. I'll start with the income tax filings you'll have to make, which vary depending on whether you stick with pass-through tax treatment or make a special election to receive corporate tax treatment.

> CAUTION
> **Make estimated tax payments.** Your LLC's members will all have to make quarterly estimated income tax payments during the year. (Of course, if it looks like your LLC will not earn a profit and won't be allocating profits to members at the end of the year, the members probably won't have to estimate and pay income taxes to the IRS and state tax board during the year.) If you miss

making required estimated tax payments, you will be charged penalties and interest. To make quarterly tax payments, each member sends in a payment four times a year along with IRS Form 1040-ES. For details, see Publication 505, *Tax Withholding and Estimated Tax,* available at the IRS website at www.irs.gov. In some cases, the LLC itself must make quarterly estimated income tax payments. This may be the case if your state charges the LLC a separate entity-level fee or tax or if your LLC has elected corporate tax treatment.

### For LLCs With Pass-Through Tax Treatment

If you will be the only owner of your LLC, your tax returns will be relatively simple. Your LLC itself will not have to file any of its own tax forms. You'll report all of your LLC income (or losses) on your federal personal tax return. You'll also have to fill out Schedule C, *Profit or Loss From Business (Sole Proprietorship),* on which you'll report your LLC profits or losses, and attach it to your 1040 form.

If yours is a multi-owner LLC, you and your co-owners will also report your income from the LLC on your individual income tax returns, Form 1040. But in this situation, even though the LLC itself doesn't pay any income taxes, it does have to file an informational return, IRS Form 1065, each year (the same tax form used by partnerships). Form 1065 includes Schedule K, which reports the total profits, losses, credits, and deductions allocated to the owners. In addition, the LLC must prepare a Schedule K-1 for each owner, which reports that owner's share of profits, losses, and other items shown on Form 1065's Schedule K. The owners attach a copy of the Schedule K-1 to their 1040 forms, and use the information on the K-1 to report LLC profits on their individual tax returns.

### For LLCs With Corporate Tax Treatment

If your LLC elects corporate tax treatment (by filing IRS Form 8832), the IRS will treat it as a separate taxable entity. The LLC will have to file a corporate tax return, IRS Form 1120, *U.S. Corporation Income Tax Return,* and estimate and pay its own income taxes at the appropriate corporate tax rate.

RESOURCE

**Get tax forms online.** You can get the tax forms mentioned above from the IRS website. Go to www.irs.gov and click on "Forms and Pubs." There you can print blank forms to be filled in by hand or typewriter, or even insert your information into a form and print it out. Some companies can now file their forms electronically—browse the IRS website if you're interested.

## State Taxes

Most states follow the federal lead and classify your LLC the same way the IRS does. This normally means that, unless you file IRS Form 8832 to elect corporate tax treatment, your LLC will be treated as a pass-through entity at the state level. Just as with the IRS, the members themselves will pay state income taxes on LLC profits and salaries (assuming your state has a personal income tax). However, even if your LLC itself won't be subject to state entity-level income taxes, it may have to file a state informational return or submit a copy of its federal tax return to the state business tax office.

TIP

**Some states charge an annual LLC fee or tax.** A handful of states, including California, charge an annual entity-level fee or tax, regardless of the LLC's income tax status. In some of these states, the fee is a flat yearly amount; in others it is graduated, depending on the gross income or net profits of the LLC; in yet others, it's both. Contact your state's department of taxation or franchise tax board for details. (See Appendix A for how to locate the tax office website address for your state.)

If your LLC will have to pay a state franchise tax or state income taxes, it may have to make estimated state tax payments. Like federal income taxes, state franchise or income taxes usually must be prepaid in four installments during the tax year, with the first payment consisting of any minimum amount charged. If the LLC doesn't make estimated tax payments, it will be charged penalties and interest. In some states, your LLC status can be suspended if the LLC fails to pay these state taxes for a few years.

## Employment Tax Filings

A multi-member LLC will need to obtain a federal Employer Identification Number (EIN) using IRS Form SS-4 and register as an employer in your state. For salaried workers, your LLC must withhold, report, and pay:

- federal and, if applicable, state income taxes
- federal employment taxes (unemployment, Social Security, and Medicare taxes), and
- state payroll taxes (state unemployment, disability, and workers' compensation insurance).

LLC members who receive a share of LLC profits are not normally treated as employees, but the LLC must withhold income tax on any guaranteed payments made to members. Ask your tax adviser if you have questions.

A single-owner LLC can typically use the owner's Social Security number as its tax ID, rather than getting an EIN. However, the LLC will need a separate EIN if it has employees or sets up a 401(k) or other type of qualified plan. Check the IRS website (www.irs.gov) and ask a tax professional for current information.

## Other State and Local Tax Filings

State sales tax, use tax, and county property tax payments apply to LLCs. Counties and cities also may impose local and regional taxes. Check with your county and city tax offices for current information on reporting and payment requirements.

## Signing LLC Paperwork Properly

Most owners who form an LLC do so to avoid personal liability for business debts and claims, at least in part. To help make sure you and other LLC members keep your limited liability legal protection, members should always sign LLC papers, documents, contracts, and other commitments clearly in the name of the LLC, not in their own names.

The best way to do this is to first state the name of the LLC, then sign your name on its behalf.

> **EXAMPLE:** Tom is one of two members of Park Place Plasterers, LLC. He enters into a long-term contract for the refurbishing of apartments in a high-rise condominium. Tom signs the contract as follows:
>
> Date: November 3, 2017
>
> Park Place Plasterers, LLC
>
> By: _____*Tom Park*_____ ,
>       Tom Park, Member

If you sign contracts in your own name without making it clear that you're acting for your LLC, as illustrated above, there's a chance you could be held personally liable to carry out the contract you've signed if the LLC can't. For example, you might have to pay money if the LLC goes broke. To be on the safe side, make this simple signing procedure a regular part of your standard day-to-day LLC business routine.

# Securities Filings

**SKIP AHEAD**
**One-member LLCs normally don't have to worry about securities law issues.** If you will be the lone member of your LLC and don't plan to take investments from outsiders, your membership interest should not be considered a security and you can skip ahead to Chapter 7. Securities laws are meant to protect investors from unscrupulous business operators; they are not meant to protect active business owners from the consequences of their own business activities.

As I discussed in Chapter 3, the initial members of an LLC ordinarily make financial contributions to the business to get it started. Commonly, all initial members will be active in working for and managing the business. But sometimes, the LLC will solicit capital (funding) from outside investors, meaning there may be some LLC members who do not manage or work in the business. Either way, when someone buys into an LLC (whether as a working member or an outside investor) for a share of its profits, that person purchases a membership interest in the business. The question we need to focus on here is: Is a membership interest in an LLC, and more specifically, in your LLC, considered a "security" within the meaning of state and federal law? If the answer is "Yes," your membership interests must either be:

- registered at the federal level (with the Securities and Exchange Commission—SEC) and with your state securities office, or
- eligible for an exemption from federal and state securities registration requirements.

If the answer is "No"—membership interests in your LLC do not fit within the definition of "securities"—you won't have to worry about seeking an exemption from securities registration rules or registering them.

## Are LLC Membership Interests Securities?

Like LLCs themselves, the question of whether and under what circumstances LLC membership interests may be treated as securities is relatively new, which means that federal and state laws are in a state of development on this point. Generally speaking, however, when LLC owners rely on their own efforts to make a profit, their membership interests are normally not considered securities under federal and state law. On the other hand, if someone invests in a business with the expectation of making money from *others'* efforts, federal and state statutes, as well as the courts, usually treat that owner's membership interest as a security.

## Member-Managed LLCs

If you and your co-owners plan to set up a member-managed LLC—which, by definition, will be actively managed by all members—your membership interests should not be treated as securities. Why? Because by actively managing your LLC, you and your co-owners are expecting to profit from your own efforts, not just from the efforts of others (if you have employees, the fact that you may profit from their work doesn't matter in this context). Even if you or your co-owners don't plan to work in the business on a daily basis, you should be considered active owners under the securities laws if you plan to be active in business management. For example, if you are setting up a small LLC with your spouse (say a car repair service), and one of you plans to manage the business end of it while the other will work in the service department from 9 to 5, you're probably safe deciding that your LLC is exempt from securities laws.

Some states have enacted legislation that codifies this rule. These statutes say that if all LLC members actively participate in LLC management, their membership interests are not securities under state law. But in a few states with such statutes, "actively participating in management" is interpreted strictly. For example, California statutes say that it is not enough for an LLC's members to have the right to vote or participate in management—an LLC must be able to prove that all of its members truly participate in the company on a regular basis or it will have to comply with securities laws.

Even if you don't live in California or another state with similar rules, it's best to insist that your members measure up to this strict participation standard. If you want to be sure your membership interests will never be treated as securities, all members, new and old, should actively participate in LLC management. If this won't be the case, your safest tack is to assume all membership interests in your LLC are securities and move on to "Exemptions to Securities Registration Requirements," below. Likewise, if any of your members for some reason don't have the right to vote, you'd better assume your membership interests will be treated as securities.

**SEE AN EXPERT**

**See a lawyer if one or more of your LLC members wants to be inactive.** It's no joke to be out of compliance with securities laws. It could even give rise to a lawsuit down the road by a disgruntled member. So if your members will include inactive investors, even if you haven't formally set up a manager-managed LLC, see a small business lawyer for advice about whether your membership interests must be registered with the government. The interests of most small LLCs will qualify for an exemption, as explained below.

What if some members will be active participants in the LLC's management, but one or more will not? In that case, it's possible the feds and the state will treat *all* of the membership interests in the LLC as securities. Securities agencies have been known to take an all-or-nothing position: either all LLC memberships are exempt from securities laws or none are. Again, if any one of your members won't be active in your LLC, you should assume your membership interests will be treated as securities and consult with a lawyer to figure out your options.

## Manager-Managed LLCs

If you set up a manager-managed LLC, it's likely that the ownership interests of at least the nonmanaging members will be treated as securities under state and federal law. That's because these nonmanaging members won't actively participate in management, so by definition they'll expect to make a profit from the efforts of others. Nonmanaging members are usually outside investors who choose not to take a management role in your business, but wish to share in the profits of the LLC.

> **EXAMPLE:** Bert and Arnie, two chemical engineers, want to set up an LLC to market their invention, a flexible scuba-diving glove—called the "Claw"—that's made of waterproof polymers. Bert and Arnie plan to manufacture and distribute the glove themselves in their free time, with the help of a small group of employees. They invite a few coworkers at their chemical plant to invest in their new part-time business, but they make it clear that anyone who invests money won't be taking part in the day-to-day management

decisions of the company (the coworkers will be nonmanaging members). Bert and Arnie are about to set up their LLC and issue membership interests to themselves and the initial investment group. Should they talk with a securities lawyer before talking to and taking any money from their coworkers? Yes. The membership interests that Bert and Arnie will sell to their coworkers meet the definition of securities, because the coworkers will not actively participate in the business and will expect to make profits from Bert and Arnie's work. Before Bert and Arnie sell the membership interests to their coworkers, they'll have to make sure the issuance of these membership interests will be exempt under state and federal securities laws or they'll have to register them.

Of course, the interests of the managing members of a manager-managed LLC will probably not, on their own, be considered securities—the managers will be considered active owners under the securities laws. But remember, securities agencies usually take an all-or-nothing position on this issue. Anytime you plan to bring in a new LLC member who won't take an active role, you should make sure your LLC fits into one of the exemptions discussed just below or you may have to register the membership interests as securities.

## Exemptions to Securities Registration Requirements

So far, I've talked about the definition of securities and why it's important to understand the issues, but I haven't told you why the securities laws exist in the first place. They do serve a purpose—namely, to ensure that people who are considering investing in a business (without managing it) are aware of any foreseeable risks associated with the business. They do this by making sure that the company discloses all relevant information on the company's risks to potential investors and that the investors are in a position to make an educated decision. Some states, like California, even require that all sales of securities be generally fair to all of the investors.

TIP

**Make full disclosure your motto when taking money from investors.** There is one basic provision of both federal and state law that applies to all securities transactions: provide full and fair disclosure of all relevant information, financial and otherwise. You should follow this rule regardless of whether your membership interests will be treated as securities or not. But particularly if you solicit investments from outsiders, disclose in writing all of the known and foreseeable risks of investing in your enterprise, and make all of your financial records fully available. If you go out of your way to disclose everything you know about your company, you'll stand a much better chance of fending off securities law problems later if your business does poorly and a member-investor becomes dissatisfied about the LLC's lower-than-expected profits.

But in some instances where potential investors are in a position to protect themselves—usually because of their past investment history or acquaintance with the business owners—the law says that the sale of interests in an LLC need not be fully registered. This is where exemptions to the securities law come in. The exemptions define the situations where federal and state securities agencies either do not register the sale of the securities or do so minimally. If you think your membership interests may be considered securities, your next step is to see whether they'll fall into one of these exemptions from the registration requirements.

Below is a summary of the most commonly relied-upon exemptions from the federal securities law. Many states either defer to or adopt these federal exemptions in their securities laws, so if the sale of your membership interests will fit under a federal exemption, it may also fit under a state exemption.

## Private Offering Exemption

Under federal case law (law developed in the courts), as well as the securities laws of many states, a private sale of securities, without advertising or promotion, to a limited number of people (usually no more than 35) is often eligible for a "private offering" exemption.

Typically, you stand a better chance of being eligible for this exemption if you only sell membership interests in your LLC to a limited number of people who either have a close family or business relationship with you or one of your co-owners or have enough investment savvy to be able to protect themselves. Also, your investors should be buying the membership interests for themselves (that is, not for resale to other investors), and they shouldn't be able to transfer their membership interests freely. For example, you can place language restricting the further transfer of a membership interest right on the membership certificate, and you can make a conspicuous notation in the LLC records that your membership interests are nontransferable.

A typical statement that limits the transfer of membership interests reads like this:

> THE SECURITIES REPRESENTED BY THIS CERTIFICATE HAVE NOT BEEN QUALIFIED OR REGISTERED UNDER ANY STATE OR FEDERAL SECURITIES LAW, AND THEY MAY NOT BE TRANSFERRED OR OTHERWISE DISPOSED OF WITHOUT SUCH QUALIFICATION OR REGISTRATION PURSUANT TO SUCH LAWS OR AN OPINION OF LEGAL COUNSEL SATISFACTORY TO THE ISSUER THAT SUCH QUALIFICATION OR REGISTRATION IS NOT REQUIRED.

**TIP**

**This informal private offering exemption works for many small LLCs.** Passive investors in many smaller LLCs will fit within this traditional securities law exemption. Why? Because in a typical small LLC, memberships are issued to a limited number of people, memberships are a personal investment by the members, and the transfer of membership interests to outsiders is restricted under the LLC operating agreement.

> **EXAMPLE:** Value Added Ventures, LLC, is started by three active members, who work full time in the business. In need of cash after their first year in business, they obtain $100,000 in investment capital from Joe, a mutual friend and business acquaintance, who

will be a nonmanaging member. The LLC has now sold a total of four membership interests: one each to the three founders, and one to the nonmanaging investor, Joe.

When the three initial active members started their LLC, they felt comfortable that their LLC membership interests were not securities—after all, all three founders planned to work in the business. But when they considered taking an investment from Joe, they weren't so sure. If Joe planned to work in the business, or help manage it, that would be one thing—Joe's interest probably wouldn't be considered a security. But Joe had no interest in doing either, so they worried that they might be about to sell a security. Before Joe was brought in, the initial members retained a small business lawyer to make sure the sale qualified under an exemption from federal and state securities laws. They did this even though they planned to disclose all financial information and risks of the business to Joe, and even though they were on close terms with him. In case their business didn't do well and Joe became disgruntled, as long as they had complied with the securities laws, Joe wouldn't be able to sue them for the return of his money by claiming a technical securities violation. Fortunately, their lawyer assured them that they could safely rely on the private offering exemption for both federal law and their state's securities law.

### Regulation D Exemption

If you want an extra level of certainty when issuing memberships in your LLC to outsiders, your LLC might decide to use federal "Regulation D." Regulation D is really a more complicated version of the private offering exemption, but it requires you to file formal exemption paperwork. To use Regulation D, you must follow the requirements contained in the federal Regulation D statute, and file Form D with the Securities and Exchange Commission (SEC).

Generally, you stand a good chance of qualifying under Regulation D if you privately offer and sell membership interests (without advertising or promotion) to 35 or fewer people, who, because of significant investment experience or personal net worth, can reasonably be assumed to be able to protect themselves. In addition, your membership interests must not be freely transferable—that is, you must place restrictions on the further transfer of your LLC memberships, as explained in the private offering exemption, above.

> **EXAMPLE:** Let's revisit the Value Added Ventures LLC. Assume that, instead of taking an investment from their friend Joe, the three original, active members cast a wider net looking for investment capital. They find a venture capital group consisting of five affluent investors willing to invest $500,000 in their LLC. Their LLC lawyer again believes that the issuance of these membership interests will be exempt from securities registration. There are fewer than 35 investors, and all of them are sophisticated, professional investors with a lot of assets. While the issuance of these membership interests could probably still be eligible for the private offering exemption, their lawyer recommends filing for a federal Regulation D exemption to be on the safe side. The lawyer has each investor sign an investment letter certifying he or she meets the accredited investor requirements of the Regulation D rules, is purchasing the investment for his or her own account, assumes the risk of the investment, has read and received all financial statements necessary to make an informed decision, and understands that the resale of memberships is restricted under the federal and state securities laws. A notice under Regulation D is filed with the SEC and the state securities agency, and copies of the investment letters and the notice form are placed in the LLC records.

Many states also recognize this exemption, so that if a securities transaction complies with federal Regulation D, it may also qualify for a state exemption.

### One-State Sales

There is another exemption that may be available under the federal securities laws (but not under state law). Called the "intrastate offering exemption," contained in Section 3(a)(11) of the Securities Act, this one exempts the offer and sale of securities made within one state only. So if you privately offer and sell memberships within your state and only to residents of your state, you may qualify for this federal exemption. Even though you wouldn't need to make a filing with the federal SEC if you qualify for this exemption, you will need to qualify for a state exemption or register the sale with the securities agency in the state where you will sell securities.

 **TIP**

**You'll have to look into state securities law exemptions too.** In some states, you may need to file a form to qualify for an exemption from state securities requirements, often along with a filing fee. To learn about state securities rules that may affect you, you can check your state securities laws online. (See Appendix A for information.) From your state's security agency website, you should be able to quickly link to a security exemption page on the site that lists any exemptions that apply to private security offerings in your state. Normally, it takes just a few minutes to locate your state's private placement exemption (or a similar "small" or "limited" offering exemption) and to read the section of the law that contains its requirements. As an alternative, you can call your state's securities board or similar agency and ask for a copy of the state laws and regulations that deal with the sale of LLC membership interests. Of course, you may not be able to decipher the legalese, in which case I suggest spending an hour or so with a lawyer to make sure you understand the rules.

After finding out about the federal and state exemptions available, you must decide whether to rely on the private placement exemption or file for a formal exemption. This decision should be a legal and practical one that you make based on your own personal comfort level in this area of law and the particular facts of your LLC.

SEE AN EXPERT

**Talking to a lawyer is your best bet.** Securities laws are murky, and the newness of the LLC throws a little extra mud in the water. If you're not sure whether you're required by law to either qualify for an exemption or register your membership interests as securities, consider spending some time with a lawyer to get some professional advice—brainstorming with an LLC lawyer to come up with a safe securities law approach should be well worth the legal fees necessary to put this technical issue to rest. Not an inexpensive solution, but one that can save you money in fees and court costs later.

## Securities Registration

If your membership interests are in fact securities and the sale doesn't fall under one of the above exemptions, you will have to register them with federal and state securities agencies. This is a somewhat unlikely scenario for most smaller LLCs, but if it's necessary, it makes sense to hire a lawyer to help you register. Securities laws are very complex. Because there are numerous federal and state registration procedures, it probably isn't worth your time and effort to try to do it yourself.

# Getting Legal and Tax Help for Your LLC

Throughout this book, I've flagged legal and tax issues that go beyond the scope of the book. If you are facing any of these more complex issues, consider a consultation with an experienced small business lawyer or adviser. Even if you didn't identify any areas where additional help is essential, if you plan to start an LLC of any size or complexity—or convert a good-sized existing business to LLC status—you're likely to benefit from the advice of someone who has done it many times before. And this is true even if you plan to do much of the form preparation and filing work yourself. Although getting a few hours of professional help will cost several hundred dollars, it is likely to be money well spent.

# Getting Legal Help for Your LLC

Here are suggestions on finding a good small business lawyer. First things first: What kind of lawyer should you be looking for?

## The "Legal Coach" Arrangement

Most small business owners do not want—and can't afford—a lawyer who will do all of their legal decision making and paperwork. Instead, I suggest you find a small business lawyer who's willing to be your "legal coach"—a professional who is willing to work with you, not just for you—in establishing your LLC and helping with ongoing LLC legal formalities. Under this model, the lawyer helps you take care of many routine legal matters yourself and helps you educate yourself on the basics of small business and LLC law, but is also available for short consultations—and, if necessary, help with paperwork—if more complicated legal issues arise.

### How to Find a Lawyer Who's Willing to Be Your Coach

Some lawyers are not comfortable with the "legal coach" model. For example, some lawyers won't review documents you have drafted using self-help materials, perhaps because they feel that there is not enough profit in it to justify the trouble and malpractice risk. So to save time, when you call a lawyer, make it clear that you are looking for a lawyer who will help you help yourself (for example, review a contract that you have prepared) or who can handle ongoing legal work from time to time. If the lawyer has a problem with this type of relationship, keep shopping — plenty of good lawyers are always looking for more business clients.

When you find a lawyer who seems agreeable to the arrangement you've proposed, ask if you can come in to meet for a half hour or so. At the in-person interview, discuss important issues such as the lawyer's customary charges for services, as explained below. Pay particular attention to the rapport between you and your lawyer. Remember, you are looking for a legal adviser who will work with you. Trust your instincts and seek a lawyer whose personality and business sense are compatible with your own.

## When to Use a Legal Coach

People with simple small businesses who wish to form a basic LLC can very likely do this on their own. As I have mentioned earlier, Nolo publishes *Form Your Own Limited Liability Company,* which helps you to do this at a very reasonable cost. So where might a small business coach come in? First, consider talking to your coach briefly about your conclusion that it makes sense for you to start an LLC or convert your existing business to an LLC. (And don't forget to ask your coach about the securities issues that I discussed in Chapter 6—your lawyer should be very familiar with your state securities law.) Most likely, the lawyer will confirm your conclusion and encourage you to take the next step.

With a reliable self-help resource, you should be able to draft and file your articles of organization on your own. Your next step will be to draft your longer and more complicated operating agreement. You may want to run your draft past your legal coach for a review and any suggestions on how you should fine-tune it to fit your situation.

Later, your coach will be best employed to look over and help draft important documents (such as contracts and leases) and to be available to talk to you should you experience a dispute with an employee, customer, supplier, or competitor. Obviously, the amount of work you hand over to a legal coach is up to you. Again, many small business owners find that it makes sense to gain a good working knowledge of legal basics (employment law, for example) and talk to their lawyer only when really needed. Fortunately, legal information and resources are becoming even easier to find on the Internet (see "Doing Self-Help Legal Research," below). And many small business publications and trade associations regularly publish very helpful materials.

## Finding a Lawyer

When looking for a small business lawyer, often the best approach is to ask someone you trust to be able to make an informed referral. If you can't think of an obvious person, talk to people who own or operate efficiently-run businesses of comparable size and scope to yours. Obviously, you are looking for someone who highly recommends a helpful, knowledgeable, and reasonably priced lawyer specializing in small business issues. If the businessperson you talk to has successfully formed an LLC with the help of the lawyer, so much the better. If you talk to several business people, chances are you'll come away with some good leads. And, of course, other knowledgeable people in your network, such as your banker, accountant, insurance agent, or real estate broker, may also be able to provide the names of lawyers they trust to help them with business matters.

How shouldn't you search for a lawyer? Don't just pick a name out of a phone book or advertisement—you really have no idea what you are getting. Lawyer referral services operated by bar associations are often equally unhelpful. Often, these simply supply the names of lawyers who have signed onto the service, without independently researching the skills or expertise the lawyer claims to have.

What about looking for a lawyer online? Obviously many lawyers have their own websites, and there are a number of online lawyer directories. Look for sites that do two things:

- provide in-depth biographical information about a lawyer. You want to know where the lawyer went to school, how long he or she has been in practice, the lawyer's specialties, and whether the lawyer has published articles or books on small business law or is a member of relevant trade organizations.

- provide helpful information about how a lawyer likes to practice. For example, if a lawyer's biographical information states that he or she enjoys helping small business owners understand the legal information they need to actively participate in solving their own legal problems, you may wish to set up an appointment.

**RESOURCE**

**Check out Nolo's lawyer directory.** Nolo maintains a lawyer directory on its website, www.nolo.com, which provides detailed profiles of listed lawyers.

## Paying for a Lawyer

Few small business owners can afford to buy all the legal information they need at $200–$300 per hour or more. The fact that you are reading this book shows that you understand how to obtain high-quality legal information on your own. Most likely, you will use a lawyer only when you really require his or her specialized negotiating, drafting, or litigating skills. For most day-to-day legal concerns, you only need a legal coach or mentor adept at helping you help yourself, not someone who wants to mail you a bill every Friday.

When you approach a lawyer, it's important to be up front about money and find out exactly how and when you'll be charged. For example, if you call the lawyer from time to time for general advice or to be steered to a good information source, how will you be billed? Some lawyers charge a flat amount for a call or a conference; others bill to the nearest 6-, 10-, or 20-minute interval. Whatever the lawyer's system, you need to understand it.

Especially at the beginning of your working relationship, when you are still a little unsure about how the lawyer operates, ask specifically about what a particular job, such as forming a limited liability company, will cost. If you feel it's too much, say so. You should be able to do some of the routine work yourself, thus reducing the fee. Even if you can afford it, it is usually unwise to pay the lawyer a hefty retainer up front—if you are not satisfied with the lawyer's work, you'll have a tough time getting even a partial refund. Far better to pay for a few hours of the lawyer's time and go from there.

Especially if you will hire a lawyer to help with a significant legal problem (for example, defend a lawsuit), it's a good idea to get your arrangement in writing. In several states, fee agreements between lawyers and clients must be in writing only if the expected fee is $1,000 or more or is contingent on the outcome of a lawsuit. But whether required or not, it's a good idea to get a written agreement.

## Using Nonlawyer Professionals

Using other types of professionals can cut down on legal costs when appropriate. Often, nonlawyer professionals perform some tasks better and at less cost than lawyers. For example, look to management consultants for strategic business planning, real estate brokers or appraisers for valuation of property, financial planners for investment advice, an experienced bookkeeper for routine financial record keeping, independent paralegals for routine form-drafting, and CPAs for the preparation of LLC tax returns. Each of these matters is likely to have a legal aspect, and eventually it's possible you'll want to consult your lawyer. But at the very least, you'll use a lot less lawyer time—and probably save some money—if you get as much information as possible from nonlawyer professionals first.

A few words about the "independent paralegal" are in order. Sometimes called legal document preparers, these nonlawyer professionals specialize in helping nonlawyers prepare routine legal forms such as those needed for divorce, bankruptcy, or organizing a business. In a number of states, including California, Florida, and Arizona, these services are readily available for a fraction of what lawyers charge. In others, they may be harder to find. Working with an independent paralegal to form an LLC can make sense as long as you are conversant with all of the legal issues and are looking for reasonably priced help with form preparation only. But because independent paralegals cannot provide in-depth legal information, they are not a good substitute for lawyers. And, of course, if you are willing to do the form preparation yourself, you can save even the paralegal's fee.

## Doing Self-Help Legal Research

Law is information, not magic. If you can look up necessary information yourself, you need not purchase it from a lawyer. Finding basic LLC law is not difficult. You can do much of the research necessary to understand your state's LLC act online. Of course, interpreting typically obtuse legal language can be difficult, so if important issues are involved, it can make sense to check your conclusions with a lawyer. Or if you have the energy and time, you can read one of the professional practice manuals lawyers often rely on.

In doing broad legal research for your business, there are a number of sources for legal rules, procedures, and issues that you may wish to examine. Here are a few:

- **State limited liability company statutes.** These state laws—your state's LLC act—should be your primary source of the rules for organizing and operating your LLC.
- **Other state laws, such as the corporations, partnerships, securities, commercial, civil, labor, and revenue codes.** These and other laws govern the operation of other types of businesses or specific business transactions; the content, approval, and enforcement of commercial contracts; employment practices and procedures; employment tax requirements; and other aspects of doing business in your state. Depending on the type of business you run, you also may want to research statutes and regulations dealing with legal topics such as environmental law, products liability, real estate, copyrights, and so on.
- **Federal laws.** These include the tax laws and procedures found in the Internal Revenue Code and the Treasury Regulations that implement these code sections; regulations dealing with advertising, warranties, and other consumer matters adopted by the Federal Trade Commission; and equal opportunity statutes such as Title VII of the Civil Rights Act.

- **Administrative rules and regulations (issued by federal and state administrative agencies charged with implementing statutes).** State and federal statutes are often supplemented with regulations that clarify specific statutes and contain rules for an agency to follow in implementing and enforcing them. For example, most states have enacted special administrative regulations under their securities statutes that provide exemptions for businesses registering the offer and sale of interests to others within the state.

- **Secondary sources.** Also important in researching business law are sources that provide background information on particular areas of law. One example is this book. Others are commonly found in the business, legal, or reference section of your local library or bookstore (for example, see Nolo's small business titles in the next section).

## Nolo Small Business Legal Resources

A good place to start when you have a legal question is always Nolo's website, www.nolo.com. It contains lots of free, helpful information on all sorts of business tasks. For instance, in the small business section, you'll find information on limited liability, financing, accounting, and contracts. Also on Nolo's website you can check our answers to Frequently Asked Questions (FAQs)—a collection of answers to over 1,000 of the questions our customers ask most often.

For further information, below are several products available from Nolo that offer valuable business information for LLC owners:

- **Nolo's online LLC formation service.** Helps you form your LLC directly on the Internet. Once you pick a package and complete an interview online, Nolo will create a customized LLC operating agreement for your LLC and file your articles of organization with the state filing office (your LLC will come into existence the day the articles are filed). To form your LLC online or get more information, go to www.nolo.com/online-LLC.

- *Form Your Own Limited Liability Company,* by Anthony Mancuso. This book provides a full treatment of LLC laws and requirements. It contains step-by-step instructions for preparing articles and an LLC operating agreement to form an LLC in your state, as well as extensive legal and tax background information.

- *Your Limited Liability Company: An Operating Manual*, by Anthony Mancuso. Provides ready-to-use minutes forms for holding formal LLC meetings and contains forms and information for formally approving legal, tax, and other important business decisions that arise in the course of operating an LLC.

- *Business Buyout Agreements: Plan Now for All Types of Business Transitions,* by Anthony Mancuso and Bethany K. Laurence. This book shows you how to adopt comprehensive buy-sell provisions to handle the purchase and sale of ownership interests in an LLC when an owner withdraws, dies, becomes disabled, or wishes to sell an interest to an outsider. Comes with an easy-to-use agreement— simply check the appropriate options, then fill in the blanks.

- *Tax Savvy for Small Business,* by Frederick W. Daily and Jeffrey A. Quinn. This book gives business owners basic information about federal taxes and explains how to make the best tax decisions for business, maximize profits, and stay out of trouble with the IRS.

- *The Employer's Legal Handbook: Manage Your Employees & Workplace Effectively,* by Fred S. Steingold. Here's a comprehensive resource that compiles all the basics of employment law in one place. It covers safe hiring practices, wages, hours, tips and commissions, employee benefits, taxes and liability, insurance, discrimination, sexual harassment, and termination.

- *Legal Guide for Starting & Running a Small Business,* by Fred S. Steingold. This book is an essential resource for every small business owner, whether just starting out or already established. Find out the basics about negotiating a favorable lease, hiring and firing employees, writing contracts, and resolving business disputes.

- *Negotiate the Best Lease for Your Business,* by Fred S. Steingold and Janet Portman. Most businesses need a space to work out of, and this book helps you find that space and negotiate a favorable lease.

# Getting Tax Help

As I discuss in detail in Chapter 4, forming an LLC requires you to understand and choose among various tax options. For example, you will have to determine whether you want your LLC to be taxed on a pass-through basis or whether it might make sense—now or later—to elect corporate tax treatment instead. Other LLC business decisions involve tax-related issues such as selecting a tax year and accounting period, setting up appropriate bookkeeping procedures, withholding and reporting payroll taxes, preparing tax returns, and scheduling distributions of profits and losses to LLC members. Accomplishing these tasks and making informed decisions in these and other tax areas may require help from a tax adviser. How do you find one?

## Finding an LLC Tax Adviser

Like locating a knowledgeable small business lawyer, the best way to find a tax adviser is to shop around for someone recommended by small business people whose judgment you trust. Your tax person should be available over the phone to answer routine questions, or by mail, fax, or email to handle paperwork and correspondence, with a minimum of formality. It is likely that you will spend much more time dealing with your tax adviser than your legal adviser, so be particularly attentive to the personal side of this relationship.

LLC tax issues are often cloudy and subject to a range of inter-pretations and strategies, so it is absolutely essential that you discuss and agree on the level of tax-aggressiveness you expect from your adviser. Some LLC owners prefer to live on the tax edge, saving every possible tax dollar. Others are content to steer a middle course—forgoing the most aggressive tax strategies in exchange for an extra measure of peace of mind. Whatever your tax strategy, make sure you find a tax adviser who feels the same way you do or is willing to defer to your more aggressive or conservative tax tendencies.

## Other LLC Tax Resources

Your tax adviser isn't your only resource for tax and financial issues. For example, banks can be an excellent source of general financial advice. After all, a bank that is a creditor of your LLC has a stake in the success of your business. The Small Business Administration's website (www.sba.gov) is another good source of financial and tax information and resources.

The IRS publishes a number of helpful publications. You can pick these up at your local IRS office, download them from the IRS website (www.irs.gov), or call the toll-free IRS forms and publications request telephone number at 800-TAX-FORM. Here are several I recommend:

- IRS Publication 509, *Tax Calendars.* This pamphlet contains a tax calendar showing important dates for business and employer filings during the year.
- IRS Publication 15, *Circular E, Employer's Tax Guide*, and the Publication 15-A Supplement, as well as IRS Publication 334, *Tax Guide for Small Business (For Individuals Who Use Schedule C or C-EZ).* You can find further information on withholding, depositing, reporting, and paying federal employment taxes in these publications. For information on providing benefits to yourself and your employees, see IRS Publication 15-B, *Employer's Tax Guide to Fringe Benefits.*
- IRS Publication 538, *Accounting Periods and Methods*, and IRS Publication 583, *Starting a Business and Keeping Records.* These publications provide helpful information on accounting methods and bookkeeping procedures.

**RESOURCE**

**More information on tax issues.** Unfortunately, many books and articles that cover LLCs and LLC taxation are not written in plain English, and do a poor job of explaining the basic terms and concepts necessary to understand the material they cover. One exception is Prentice Hall's book *Federal Taxation 2017: Comprehensive,* updated annually. It is used primarily as a text for business students, and may be available at a local business or law library. Although this book is rather advanced (and it's not cheap), it should give you a good handle on small business accounting and taxes in general.

# State Information

T he websites listed below can provide you with information about the legal and tax rules for forming and operating an LLC in your state.

## Business Entity Filing Office

This is the state office where you file your paperwork (articles or a similar document) to form an LLC or a corporation, limited partnership, or other state-regulated business. You can also contact this office, either online or by calling the telephone number provided on the site, to check the availability of your proposed business entity name and to reserve your name. State filing office websites typically provide downloadable articles forms, forms to reserve a business name, and the latest filing fee information.

To find your state's business entity filing office website, go to www.statelocalgov.net. In the left pane, choose "SOS" (for secretary of state) on the pull-down menu in the "Select Topic" box for a list of links to state offices. On your state's secretary of state website, you might need to search the tabs and menus to find the information you need on filing. Another good online resource for filing and tax offices—as well as state statutes—is Wyoming's "50 States' Information" page at http://soswy. state.wy.us/Business/Business50.aspx.

## Tax Office

This is the state's taxing authority, where you can find state LLC and corporate tax information and forms. Most states collect an annual corporate income or franchise tax, and some states impose an annual LLC tax or fee.

To find your state's tax office website, go to the Federation of Tax Administrators website, at www.taxadmin.org. Select "State Tax Agencies" under the "Taxpayers & Preparers" tab.

# Securities Office

This is the state agency where you can find information and forms for complying with your state's securities laws requirements when selling interests in your LLC, corporation, or other business entity. Most states provide an exemption from state securities registration requirements for the initial issuing of shares by a small corporation to a limited number of investors.

To find your state's securities office website, go to the North American Securities Administrators Association website at www.nasaa.org. Click on "Contact Your Regulator," then click on your state.

# Sample Operating Agreement

# Operating Agreement
## of
## Sample LLC,
## a Member-Managed Limited Liability Company

## A. Preliminary Provisions

### 1. Effective Date

This Operating Agreement of Sample LLC, effective on the date of signing, is adopted by the members whose signatures appear at the end of this agreement.

### 2. Formation

This limited liability company (LLC) was formed by filing Articles of Organization, a Certificate of Formation, or a similar organizational document with the state of California's LLC filing office on January 1, 2012. Unless a delayed effective date was specified when the Articles, Certificate of Formation, or similar document was filed, the legal existence of this LLC commenced on the date of such filing. A copy of this organizational document has been placed in the LLC's records book.

### 3. Name

The formal name of this LLC is as stated above. However, this LLC may do business under a different name by complying with the state's fictitious or assumed business name statutes and procedures.

### 4. Registered Office and Registered Agent

The registered office address of this LLC is:

55 El Portal Avenue

Portola, California 94567

The registered agent of this LLC is:

Otto Mann

The registered agent and/or office of this LLC may be changed from time to time as the members may see fit, by filing a change of registered agent or office statement with the state LLC filing office. It will not be necessary to amend this provision of the Operating Agreement if and when such changes are made.

## 5. Business Purpose

The specific business purposes and activities contemplated by the founders of this LLC at the time of initial signing of this agreement consist of the following: Operate an automotive parts supply store.

It is understood that the foregoing statement of powers shall not serve as a limitation on the powers or abilities of this LLC, which shall be permitted to engage in any and all lawful business activities. If this LLC intends to engage in business activities outside the state of its formation that require the qualification of the LLC in other states, it shall obtain such qualification before engaging in such out-of-state activities.

## 6. Duration of LLC

The duration of this LLC shall be perpetual. This LLC shall terminate when a proposal to dissolve the LLC is adopted by the membership of this LLC or when this LLC is otherwise terminated in accordance with law.

## B. Membership Provisions

### 1. Nonliability of Members

No member of this LLC shall be personally liable for the expenses, debts, obligations, or liabilities of the LLC, or for claims made against it.

### 2. Reimbursement for Organizational Costs

Members shall be reimbursed by the LLC for organizational expenses paid by the members. The LLC shall be authorized to elect to deduct organizational expenses and start-up expenditures and amortize as permitted by the Internal Revenue Code and as may be advised by the LLC's tax adviser.

3. **Management**

   This LLC shall be managed exclusively by all of its members.

4. **Members' Capital Interests**

   A member's capital interest in this LLC shall be computed as a fraction, the numerator of which is the total of a member's capital account and the denominator of which is the total of all capital accounts of all members.

5. **Membership Voting**

   Except as otherwise may be required by the Articles of Organization, Certificate of Formation, or a similar organizational document; other provisions of this Operating Agreement; or under the laws of this state; each member shall vote on any matter submitted to the membership for approval by the managers of this LLC in proportion to the member's capital interest in this LLC. Further, unless otherwise stated in another provision of this Operating Agreement, the phrase "majority of members" means a majority of members whose combined capital interests in this LLC represent more than 50% of the capital interests of all members in this LLC, and a majority of members, so defined, may approve any item of business brought before the membership for a vote.

6. **Compensation**

   Members shall not be paid as members of the LLC for performing any duties associated with such membership, including management of the LLC. Members may be paid, however, for any services rendered in any other capacity for the LLC, whether as officers, employees, independent contractors, or otherwise.

7. **Members' Meetings**

   The LLC shall not provide for regular members' meetings. However, any member may call a meeting by communicating his or her wish to schedule a meeting to all other members. Such notification may be in person or in writing, or by telephone, facsimile machine, or other form of electronic communications reasonably expected to be received by a member, and the other members shall then agree, either personally, in writing, or by telephone, facsimile machine, or other form of electronics communication to the member calling the meeting, to meet at a mutually acceptable time and place. Notice of the business to be transacted at the meeting need not be given to members by the member calling the meeting, and any business may be discussed and conducted at the meeting.

If all members cannot attend a meeting, it shall be postponed to a date and time when all members can attend, unless all members who do not attend have agreed in writing to the holding of the meeting without them. If a meeting is postponed, and the postponed meeting cannot be held either because all members do not attend the postponed meeting or the nonattending members have not signed a written consent to allow the postponed meeting to be held without them, a second postponed meeting may be held at a date and time announced at the first postponed meeting. The date and time of the second postponed meeting shall also be communicated to any members not attending the first postponed meeting. The second postponed meeting may be held without the attendance of all members as long as a majority of the capital interests of the membership of this LLC is in attendance at the second postponed meeting. Written notice of the decisions or approvals made at this second postponed meeting shall be mailed or delivered to each nonattending member promptly after the holding of the second postponed meeting.

Written minutes of the discussions and proposals presented at a members' meeting, and the votes taken and matters approved at such meeting, shall be taken by one of the members or a person designated at the meeting. A copy of the minutes of the meeting shall be placed in the LLC's records book after the meeting.

8. **Membership Certificates**
This LLC shall be authorized to obtain and issue certificates representing or certifying membership interests in this LLC. Each certificate shall

show the name of the LLC and the name of the member, and shall state that the person named is a member of the LLC and is entitled to all the rights granted members of the LLC under the Articles of Organization, Certificate of Formation, or a similar organizational document; this Operating Agreement; and provisions of law. Each membership certificate shall be consecutively numbered and signed by each of the current members of this LLC. The certificates shall include any additional information considered appropriate for inclusion by the members on membership certificates.

In addition to the above information, all membership certificates shall bear a prominent legend on their face or reverse side stating or summarizing any transfer restrictions that apply to memberships in this LLC under the Articles of Organization, Certificate of Formation, or a similar organizational document, and/or this Operating Agreement, and the address where a member may obtain a copy of these restrictions upon request from this LLC.

The records book of this LLC shall contain a list of the names and addresses of all persons to whom certificates have been issued, show the date of issuance of each certificate, and record the date of all cancellations or transfers of membership certificates by members or the LLC.

9. **Other Business by Members**

   Each member shall agree not to own an interest in, manage, or work for another business, enterprise, or endeavor, if such ownership or activities would compete with this LLC's business goals, mission, profitability, or productivity, or would diminish or impair the member's ability to provide maximum effort and performance in accomplishing the business objectives and, if applicable, managing the business of this LLC.

10. **Admission of New Members**

    Except as otherwise provided in this agreement, a person or entity shall not be admitted into membership in this LLC unless each member consents in writing to the admission of the new member. The admission of new members into this LLC who have been transferred, or wish to be transferred, a membership interest in this LLC by an existing member of this LLC is covered by separate provisions in this Operating Agreement.

## C. Tax and Financial Provisions

### 1. Tax Classification of LLC

The members of this LLC intend that this LLC be initially classified as a partnership for federal and, if applicable, state income tax purposes. It is understood that all members may agree to change the tax treatment of this LLC by signing, or authorizing the signature of, IRS Form 8832, *Entity Classification Election*, and filing it with the IRS and, if applicable, the state tax department within the prescribed time limits.

### 2. Tax Year and Accounting Method

The tax year of this LLC shall end on the last day of the month of December. The LLC shall use the cash method of accounting. Both the tax year and the accounting period of the LLC may be changed with the consent of all members if the LLC qualifies for such change, and may be effected by the filing of appropriate forms with the IRS and state tax offices.

### 3. Tax Matters Partner

If this LLC is required under Internal Revenue Code provisions or regulations, it shall designate from among its members a "tax matters partner" in accordance with Internal Revenue Code Section 6231(a)(7) and corresponding regulations, who will fulfill this role by being the spokesperson for the LLC in dealings with the IRS as required under the Internal Revenue Code and Regulations, and who will report to the members on the progress and outcome of these dealings.

4. **Annual Income Tax Returns and Reports**

Within 60 days after the end of each tax year of the LLC, a copy of the LLC's state and federal income tax returns for the preceding tax year shall be mailed or otherwise provided to each member of the LLC, together with any additional information and forms necessary for each member to complete his or her individual state and federal income tax returns. This additional information shall include a federal (and, if applicable, state) Schedule K-1 (Form 1065–*Partner's Share of Income, Deductions, Credits, etc.*) or equivalent income tax reporting form, as well as a financial report, which shall include a balance sheet and profit and loss statement for the prior tax year of the LLC.

5. **Bank Accounts**

The LLC shall designate one or more banks or other institutions for the deposit of the funds of the LLC, and shall establish savings, checking, investment, and other such accounts as are reasonable and necessary for its business and investments. One or more members of the LLC shall be designated with the consent of all members to deposit and withdraw funds of the LLC, and to direct the investment of funds from, into, and among such accounts. The funds of the LLC, however and wherever deposited or invested, shall not be commingled with the personal funds of any members of the LLC.

6. **Title to Assets**

All personal and real property of this LLC shall be held in the name of the LLC, not in the names of individual members.

## D. Capital Provisions

1. **Capital Contributions by Members**

Members shall make the following contributions of cash, property, or services to the LLC, on or by specified dates, as shown next to each member's name below. The fair market values of items of property or services as agreed between the LLC and the contributing member are also shown below.

Name of Member: Otto Mann
Description of Payment: Cash
Value of Capital Payment: $20,000
Date of Payment: January 15, 2012

Name of Member: Mike Maxwell
Description of Payment: Cash
Value of Capital Payment: $10,000
Date of Payment: January 15, 2012

## 2. Additional Contributions by Members

The members may agree, from time to time by unanimous vote, to require the payment of additional capital contributions by the members, on or by a mutually agreeable date.

## 3. Failure to Make Contributions

If a member fails to make a required capital contribution within the time agreed for a member's contribution, the remaining members may, by unanimous vote, agree to reschedule the time for payment of the capital contribution by the late-paying member, setting any additional repayment terms, such as a late payment penalty, rate of interest to be applied to the unpaid balance, or other monetary amount to be paid by the delinquent member, as the remaining members decide. Alternatively, the remaining members may, by unanimous vote, agree to cancel the membership of the delinquent member, provided any prior partial payments of capital made by the delinquent member are refunded promptly by the LLC to the member after the decision is made to terminate the membership of the delinquent member.

## 4. No Interest on Capital Contributions

No interest shall be paid on funds or property contributed as capital to this LLC, or on funds reflected in the capital accounts of the members.

5. **Capital Account Bookkeeping**

   A capital account shall be set up and maintained on the books of the LLC for each member. It shall reflect each member's capital contribution to the LLC, increased by each member's share of profits in the LLC, decreased by each member's share of losses and expenses of the LLC, and adjusted as required in accordance with applicable provisions of the Internal Revenue Code and corresponding income tax regulations.

6. **Consent to Capital Contribution Withdrawals and Distributions**

   Members shall not be allowed to withdraw any part of their capital contributions or to receive distributions, whether in property or cash, except as otherwise allowed by this agreement and, in any case, only if such withdrawal is made with the written consent of all members.

7. **Allocations of Profits and Losses**

   Except as otherwise provided in the Articles of Organization, Certificate of Formation, or a similar organizational document, or this Operating Agreement, no member shall be given priority or preference with respect to other members in obtaining a return of capital contributions, distributions, or allocations of the income, gains, losses, deductions, credits, or other items of the LLC. Except as otherwise provided in the Articles of Organization, Certificate of Formation, a similar organizational document, or this Operating Agreement, the profits and losses of the LLC, and all items of its income, gain, loss, deduction, and credit shall be allocated to members according to each member's capital interest in this LLC.

8. **Allocation and Distribution of Cash to Members**

   Cash from LLC business operations, as well as cash from a sale or other disposition of LLC capital assets, may be allocated and distributed from time to time to members in accordance with each member's capital interest in the LLC, as may be decided by a majority of the capital interests of the members.

### 9. Allocation of Noncash Distributions

If proceeds consist of property other than cash, the members shall decide the value of the property and allocate such value among the members in accordance with each member's capital interest in the LLC. If such noncash proceeds are later reduced to cash, such cash may be distributed among the members according to the distribution of cash allocations provisions in this agreement.

### 10. Allocation and Distribution of Liquidation Proceeds

Regardless of any other provision in this agreement, if there is a distribution in liquidation of this LLC, or when any member's interest is liquidated, all items of income and loss shall be allocated to the members' capital accounts, and all appropriate credits and deductions shall then be made to these capital accounts before any final distribution is made. A final distribution shall be made to members only to the extent of, and in proportion to, any positive balance in each member's capital account.

## E. Membership Withdrawal and Transfer Provisions

### 1. Withdrawal of Members

A member may withdraw from this LLC by giving written notice to all other members at least 90 days before the date the withdrawal is to be effective. In the event of such withdrawal, the LLC shall pay the departing member the fair value of his or her LLC interest, less any amounts owed by the member to the LLC. The departing and remaining members shall agree at the time of departure on the fair value of the departing member's interest and the schedule of payments to be made by the LLC to the departing member, who shall receive payment for his or her interest within a reasonable time after departure from the LLC. If the departing and remaining members cannot agree on the value of the departing member's interest, they shall select an appraiser, who shall determine the current value of the departing member's interest. This appraised amount shall be the fair value of the departing member's interest, and shall form the basis of the amount to be paid to the departing member.

2. **Restrictions on the Transfer of Membership**

Notwithstanding any other provision of this agreement, a member shall not transfer his or her membership in the LLC unless all of the nontransferring LLC members first agree in writing to approve the admission of the transferee into this LLC. Further, no member may encumber a part or all of his or her membership in the LLC by mortgage, pledge, granting of a security interest, lien, or otherwise, unless the encumbrance has first been approved in writing by all other members of the LLC.

Notwithstanding the above provision, any member shall be allowed to assign an economic interest in his or her membership to another person without the approval of the other members. Such an assignment shall not include a transfer of the member's voting or management rights in this LLC, and the assignee shall not become a member of the LLC.

## F. Dissolution Provisions

1. **Events That Trigger Dissolution of the LLC**

The following events shall trigger a dissolution of the LLC, except as provided:

a. **Dissociation of a Member.** The dissociation of a member, which means the death, incapacity, bankruptcy, retirement, resignation, or expulsion of a member, or any other event that terminates the continued membership of a member, shall cause a dissolution of this LLC only if and as provided below:

i. **If a vote must be taken under state law to avoid dissolution.** If, under provisions of state law, a vote of the remaining LLC members is required to continue the existence of this LLC after the dissociation of a member, the remaining members shall affirmatively vote to continue the existence of this LLC within the period, and by the number of votes of remaining members, that may be required under such provisions. If such a vote is required, but the period or number of votes requirement is not specified under such provisions, all remaining members must affirmatively vote to a continuation of this LLC within 90 days from the date of dissociation of the member. If the affirmative vote of the remaining members is not obtained under this provision, this LLC shall dissolve under the appropriate procedures specified under state law.

ii. **If a vote is not required under state law to avoid dissolution.** If provisions of state law do not require such a vote of remaining members to continue the existence and/or business of the LLC after the dissociation of a member, and/or allow the provisions of this Operating Agreement to take precedence over state law provisions relating to the continuance of the LLC following the dissociation of a member, then this LLC shall continue its existence and business following such dissociation of a member without the necessity of taking a vote of the remaining members. Notwithstanding the above, if the LLC is left with fewer members than required under state law for the operation of an LLC following the dissociation of a member of this LLC, the LLC shall elect or appoint a member in accordance with any provisions of state law regarding such election or appointment. If such election or appointment is not made within the time period specified under state law, or, if no time period is specified under state law and the LLC makes no election or appointment within 90 days following the date of dissociation of the member, this LLC shall dissolve under the appropriate procedures specified under state law.

b. **Expiration of LLC Term.** The expiration of the term of existence of the LLC if such term is specified in the Articles of Organization, Certificate of Formation, a similar organizational document, or this Operating Agreement, shall cause the dissolution of this LLC.

c. **Written Agreement to Dissolve.** The written agreement of all members to dissolve the LLC shall cause a dissolution of this LLC.

d. **Entry of Decree.** The entry of a decree of dissolution of the LLC under state law shall cause a dissolution of this LLC.

If the LLC is to dissolve according to any of the above provisions, the members and, if applicable, managers, shall wind up the affairs of the LLC, and take other actions appropriate to complete a dissolution of the LLC in accordance with applicable provisions of state law.

## G. General Provisions

### 1. Officers

The LLC may designate one or more officers, such as a President, Vice President, Secretary, and Treasurer. Persons who fill these positions need not be members of the LLC. Such positions may be compensated or noncompensated according to the nature and extent of the services rendered for the LLC as a part of the duties of each office. Ministerial services only as a part of any officer position will normally not be compensated, such as the performance of officer duties specified in this agreement, but any officer may be reimbursed by the LLC for out-of-pocket expenses paid by the officer in carrying out the duties of his or her office.

### 2. Records

The LLC shall keep at its principal business address a copy of all proceedings of membership meetings, as well as books of account of the LLC's financial transactions. A list of the names and addresses of the current membership of the LLC also shall be maintained at this address, with notations on any transfers of members' interests to nonmembers or persons being admitted into membership in the LLC.

Copies of the LLC's Articles of Organization, Certificate of Formation, or a similar organizational document; a signed copy of this Operating Agreement; and the LLC's tax returns for the preceding three tax years shall be kept at the principal business address of the LLC. A statement also shall be kept at this address containing any of the following information that is applicable to this LLC:

- the amount of cash or a description and value of property contributed or agreed to be contributed as capital to the LLC by each member
- a schedule showing when any additional capital contributions are to be made by members to this LLC
- a statement or schedule, if appropriate, showing the rights of members to receive distributions representing a return of part or all of members' capital contributions, and
- a description of events, or the date, when the legal existence of the LLC will terminate under provisions in the LLC's Articles of Organization, Certificate of Formation, or a similar organizational document, or this Operating Agreement.

If one or more of the above items is included or listed in this Operating Agreement, it will be sufficient to keep a copy of this agreement at the principal business address of the LLC without having to prepare and keep a separate record of such item or items at this address.

Any member may inspect any and all records maintained by the LLC upon reasonable notice to the LLC. Copying of the LLC's records by members is allowed, but copying costs shall be paid for by the requesting member.

3. **All Necessary Acts**

The members and officers of this LLC are authorized to perform all acts necessary to perfect the organization of this LLC and to carry out its business operations expeditiously and efficiently. The Secretary of the LLC, or other officers, or all members of the LLC, may certify to other businesses, financial institutions, and individuals as to the authority of one or more members or officers of this LLC to transact specific items of business on behalf of the LLC.

4. **Mediation and Arbitration of Disputes Among Members**

In any dispute over the provisions of this Operating Agreement and in other disputes among the members, if the members cannot resolve the dispute to their mutual satisfaction, the matter shall be submitted to mediation. The terms and procedure for mediation shall be arranged by the parties to the dispute.

If good-faith mediation of a dispute proves impossible or if an agreed-upon mediation outcome cannot be obtained by the members who are parties to the dispute, the dispute may be submitted to arbitration in accordance with the rules of the American Arbitration Association. Any party may commence arbitration of the dispute by sending a written request for arbitration to all other parties to the dispute. The request shall state the nature of the dispute to be resolved by arbitration, and, if all parties to the dispute agree to arbitration, arbitration shall be commenced as soon as practical after such parties receive a copy of the written request.

All parties shall initially share the cost of arbitration, but the prevailing party or parties may be awarded attorneys' fees, costs, and other expenses of arbitration. All arbitration decisions shall be final, binding, and conclusive on all the parties to arbitration, and legal judgment may be entered based upon such decision in accordance with applicable law in any court having jurisdiction to do so.

5. **Entire Agreement**

This Operating Agreement represents the entire agreement among the members of this LLC, and it shall not be amended, modified, or replaced except by a written instrument executed by all the parties to this agreement who are current members of this LLC as well as any and all additional parties who became members of this LLC after the adoption of this agreement. This agreement replaces and supersedes all prior written and oral agreements among any and all members of this LLC.

### 6. Severability

If any provision of this agreement is determined by a court or arbitrator to be invalid, unenforceable, or otherwise ineffective, that provision shall be severed from the rest of this agreement, and the remaining provisions shall remain in effect and enforceable.

## H. Signatures of Members and Spouses of Members

### 1. Execution of Agreement

In witness whereof, the members of this LLC sign and adopt this agreement as the Operating Agreement of this LLC.

Date: _____

Signature: _____ _____
               Otto Mann, Member

Date: _____ _____

Signature: _____ ___ _____
               Mike Maxwell, Member

### 2. Consent of Spouses

The undersigned, if any, are spouses of above-signed members of this LLC. These spouses have read this agreement and agree to be bound by its terms in any matter in which they have a financial interest, including restrictions on the transfer of memberships and the terms under which memberships in this LLC may be sold or otherwise transferred.

Signature: _____ _____

Signature: _____ ___ _____

# Checklist for Forming an LLC

This appendix contains a list of factors that you should consider as you decide whether it makes sense to run your business as an LLC. And assuming the answer is yes, this checklist also explains what you need to do to actually create your LLC. This list is not meant to be exhaustive. If yours is a brand-new business, you'll obviously have to take many other steps to get off the ground, including getting a business license and finding a location for your business. Because these issues are not unique to LLCs, they aren't included here.

## I. Decide If an LLC Is the Right Structure for My Business

☐ Is my type of business one in which business debts and claims could threaten my personal assets?

☐ Do I own sufficient personal assets that would be at risk (such as equity in a house) if a successful business-based lawsuit resulted in a judgment that could be collected from my personal assets?

☐ How much does my state charge to form an LLC? Does my state also charge an annual fee?

☐ How are LLCs taxed in my state? Do I have to pay an annual LLC entity franchise or income tax to my state?

☐ Is my business or profession licensed by the state? If so, will I be required to set up a professional LLC or a professional corporation instead of an LLC?

☐ Would I benefit more from forming a corporation because I plan to distribute stock options or "go public" with an IPO (initial public offering) in the future? (The benefits of incorporating are covered in Chapter 2.)

☐ Have I consulted with an accountant or lawyer to discuss any tax and legal questions about my business structure?

## II. Name My Business

☐ Choose an appropriate name for my business.

☐ Do a state and federal trademark search if necessary.

☐ Check the availability of the name with the LLC filing office.

☐ Reserve the name with the LLC filing office (for a small fee).

## III. Follow Steps Required by My State

☐ File my articles of organization (or certificate of organization or formation) with my state's LLC filing office, along with the required fee.

☐ Publish a notice of intent to form my LLC (required in some states).

☐ File a notice of bulk sales (sometimes required when converting an existing business to an LLC—see Chapter 6).

## IV. Steps to Take After Formation

☐ Prepare my LLC operating agreement.

☐ Create my LLC binder or other record-keeping system.

☐ Hold the LLC's first organizational meeting to adopt the operating agreement and elect officers (such as president and secretary). File minutes of meeting in my LLC records.

☐ File for a tax ID number (EIN) with the IRS, if required.

☐ Open an LLC bank account.

☐ Get liability insurance coverage.

## V. Ongoing Formalities

☐ Record other important ongoing decisions with minutes or written consent forms.

☐ Sign lease agreements, contracts, and loans in my LLC's name.

☐ File annual state LLC reports if required (typically for a small fee).

☐ Pay estimated tax on allocated LLC profits during the year.

☐ File annual required tax returns with the IRS and my state.

# Index